WouldArt

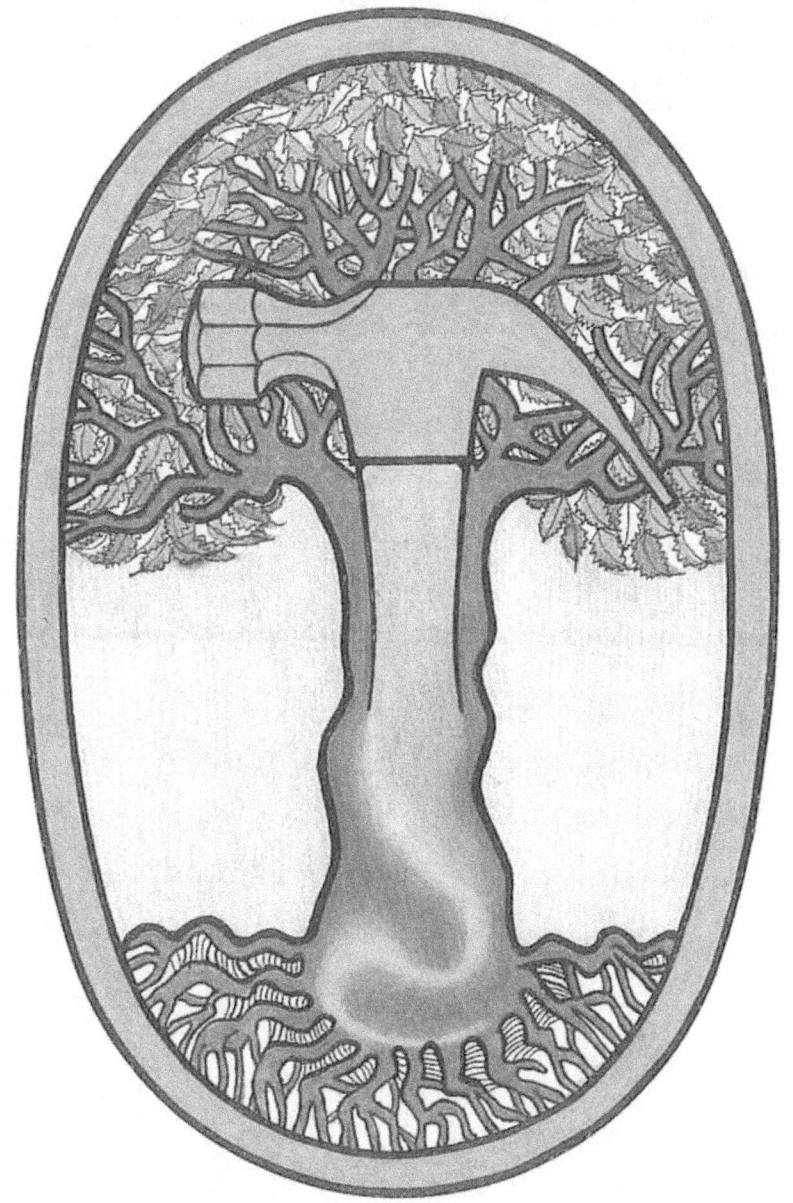

By Robert Sterler

Art By Elaine Sterler

WouldArt   HTTP://WouldArt.org

Copyright © 2006 by Robert Sterler
United States Copyright Office TX 6-370-088

All rights reserved. No part of this book shall be reproduced for commercial purposes. It is permitted to print this book locally for personnel consumption. If you wish to share this work with other; please instruct them to retrieve a free copy by registration at HTTP://WouldArt.org Reproduction and or transmitting by any means, electronic, mechanical, photocopying, recording, or otherwise, without written permission from the author is prohibited. No patent liability is assumed with respect to the use of the information contained herein. Although every precaution has been taken in the preparation of this book, the author assumes no responsibility for errors or omissions. Nor is any liability assumed for damages resulting from the use of the information contained herein.

Trademarks
All terms mentioned in this book that are known to be trademarks or service marks have been appropriately noted. The author cannot attest to the accuracy of this information. Use of a term in this book should not be regarded as affecting the validity of any trademark or service mark.

Warning and Disclaimer
Every effort has been made to make this book as complete and as accurate as possible, but no warranty or fitness is implied. The information provided is on an "as is" basis. The author shall have neither liability nor responsibility to any person or entity with respect to any loss or damages arising from the information contained in this book.

Table of Content

Acknowledgement & Dedication

Chapter one – Introduction to WouldArt

Chapter two – The Order of Things

Chapter three – Male Characteristics

Chapter four – Female Characteristics

Chapter five – Men and Women

Chapter six – Our Religions

Chapter seven – WouldArt Agenda

Chapter eight – Political Control

Chapter nine – Payoff

Acknowledgement & Dedication

I would like to acknowledge some of the people that have helped me write this book and start WouldArt. First and foremost I am indebted to my wife Susan and my daughters Sierra and Olivia. I thank them for having patience with me over this long journey. Without them I am nothing. I also am eternally grateful to my mother and father – Aimee & Bernie, who are my greatest teachers. My four sisters (Lynne, Elaine, Gail & Sharon) have and continue to help me understand women better. Tom Velasquez has helped me with editing as well as my wife Susan and my mother Aimee. My sister Elaine has worked patiently with me for over two years producing Art. Cherrone Silverman has been a stalwart supporter of the concept of WouldArt and a driving force. There are many other people who have influenced and helped me – I can not name them all. I dedicate this work to the women of tomorrow, who are not yet born, in the hope that they will carry the torch of WouldArt forward for succeeding generations of women that will live beyond them.

Chapter one

Introduction to WouldArt

WOULDART – Introduction

A rumbling is getting louder and louder on this planet. It is not, however, a physical event. Women are breaking out of the cocoon that has held them captive. Men are helping them. We are transforming as dramatically as does a butterfly. We are changing as a species in a fragile and turbulent political climate. Women's role in society is changing profoundly in relation to men. This change is causing a transformation of the human species and is significantly altering our history. Can you hear the rumble?

A chrysalis is the transformative stage a caterpillar goes through to become a butterfly, and it is a perfect metaphor for what is now happening to human beings. We are at a crucial place in human evolution in which dynamic change is inescapable. Women are leading us all in a transformation towards the next stage of our evolution, to emerge as butterflies.

The dictionary additionally defines chrysalis as "anything that is undeveloped or in a transitory state". A lot of things are changing in our world, but some changes are so huge and profound, they stand out as history making.

Four major transitions are taking place that have consequences for everyone on the planet. First is the evolution from an industrial to an information-based society. Second, regional economies are merging towards a global marketplace. Third, totalitarian governments are giving way to mass participation politics. The last and most profound is from male political supremacy to the reemergence of women in the power structure of the world. All of these great forces work and influence one another. This essay focuses primarily on the last of these great changes.

The central thesis in this work is that *women's equal participation in all aspects of society is the manifest destiny of humankind.* Equal power sharing involves a transformation from the male-dominated status quo.

Most of written history records the exclusion of women from the major decisions in society. That has been a mistake. The total human intellect is not male or female; it is both. And yet our intellect has been lopsided for thousands of years because of male-dominated policies both public and private. Men have excluded women from the halls of power. This has not been healthy for us as a species. We need to use the full range of human potential to create a synthesis of human intelligence by allowing both women (thesis) and men (antithesis) to participate.

Although the tide is changing, women are not equal participants in the culture of America and most other cultures. The imbalances in politics, religion, business, and the environment exist in large part because we are not nurturing ourselves and using our full human capabilities. We still lack substantial feminine input in the institutions that make the political, spiritual and economic decisions affecting us all. This prohibits the fulfillment of the human potential.

Women are the other half of the equation necessary to solve the problems that we face. Without their input as full and active partners in the affairs of the world we shall continue to move towards the maelstrom that we ourselves are creating.

Women - responsibility

Women have an obligation and an opportunity to change the course of human history. We must look to women, now, to transform how our systems work. This transformation is necessary for the healthy continuation of our species. This book is an exploration of feminist transformation and why it is true, necessary and inevitable. We will be focusing on women's evolution and its impact on the world as we know it. This will take us in many directions as we look at the future of humankind. Women's metamorphosis touches every corner of the human experience, and we must look at politics, psychology, economics, theology, anthropology, archeology, language, law, philosophy and the family unit. We must use all the tools at our disposal to increase our self-understanding.

Art will be used as one of the mechanisms and vehicles to present ideas – WouldArt. Art is a process of piecing elements together in an effort to make a presentation. Art usually has an intention – it wants to "say" something. Art leads us to a conclusion, understanding or appreciation. Any form of construction can be art – from words and graphic art to cooking and gardening. Art uses a variety of elements in an intentional coordination to form a message.

Wouldart uses art to induce gender equality. Wouldart is a stew of ideas and presentations that simmer together to create a digestible argument to help bring about gender equality. Wouldart can be created by one or one million persons. The ideas in this book are presented with illustrations by my sister Elaine. Her artwork is designed to reinforce a coherent message.

It is a given that nothing but change is certain, any transformation can be misdirected, truncated or delayed. Women will not automatically come to power; those of us who want women to share power equally must coordinate our energies to facilitate its emergence. The conditions and circumstances that will enable women to take hold of the reins of leadership are all here now and can be implemented if we act in concert. WouldArt asks a series of questions:

- **WouldArt Help to create Gender Equality?**
- **WouldArt be powerful to create?**
- **WouldArt be fun to do?**
- **WouldArt help us all to grow?**

The unequivocal answer to these questions is . . .   YES

Do we want or need women in leadership? The answer is that we cannot continue to exclude women from the management of this world and think that we will survive. It's not a matter of whether to include women, but rather what will happen if we don't. Men have been running the world for a long time, and, quite frankly, the world is in trouble. Most of our problems are caused, in large part, by our almost exclusive reliance on male thinking in regard to political, religious and economic decisions. The destruction of the environment and the inclination to use war to resolve differences are prime examples of male predilections. Men almost exclusively dominate our global institutions.

The question of our survival is very real. It is possible for human beings to drive themselves right out of existence, or at the very least to a very undesirable situation. To avoid that possibility we need to see ourselves as one people on Earth with a specific goal, a bright and wonderful future, and a place where we want to go. We are in the driver's seat whether we like it or not. We must understand that what we do or don't do will determine our fate. We are at a stage in human evolution in which our options for growth are limited by our decision to keep women, more than fifty percent of the world's population, out of the decision making process. It's as though we were in the middle of a chess game, some of our pieces have been lost, and our position is not good but still hopeful. We must move in bold, creative ways to insure the continuation of a healthy game for the future. The game is not man against woman or humans against nature; it is men and women with nature, in a dance towards perfection. We are the creators of tomorrow. What we do now will shape what is possible in the future.

By involving women in the decision making processes of the Earth, humankind will benefit. The ideas presented in this book will support this thesis. Many things can be done to accelerate the process of power sharing. Men must be made aware of the advantages of sharing power with women and learn how to participate in and expedite the transformation.

Men are good at reaching goals; they need to become a more integral part of the solution. Women need to be awakened and made more aware of their potential and power. Men as well as women need to become more aware of our common problems. We must understand the reasons behind our problems, and mechanisms for transformation to meet the challenges we all face.

Change is not easy for anyone; both men and women need to change. Both need help, coaxing and education in order to bring about change.

The metamorphosis of women throughout the world in social, political and economic matters of decision making cannot exclude anyone. It will have a profound and positive effect, we hope, on the planet itself and nurture all participants.

Most women have no wish to keep men from power or to place them in a state of enslavement. Reasonable men will understand that they would not be supplanted by giving women equality, but would make it possible for women to help them meet the challenges that we all face. Those who do not understand this necessary human development must be educated for the benefit of us all. We will either transform, or we will expire together.

Education - volition

In addition to educating adults about the effects of our own programming, we must search our souls for the biases we pass on to our children. Children are our future, both literally and figuratively. Children contain our hopes and desires for a better tomorrow.

As parents and elders we have a responsibility to envision a positive direction for human interactions for the

future of our world; so our children can be guided towards it. We should carefully consider what we tell children about their capabilities and what the future will be like, because tomorrow will be the outcome of how we program our children today. Our programming is the script of tomorrow's reality. Our children are tomorrow's men and women. Working together they have the potential to change the world in a positive way.

Human beings as a species are in the throes of infancy when compared to the longevity of most other animal species. If we repeat the mistakes of the past with our children, we may not make the evolutionary transition from infancy to childhood. In order to better direct ourselves we must become more knowledgeable about what compels our behavior. The changes we make in our behavior towards each other, and ourselves, will bring about a worldwide transformation. Understanding the transition process and cooperating with one another are part of the mechanics necessary to bring about that transformation. They begin with understanding the distinction between nature and nurture and recognizing the part that biology and culture play in determining human behavior.

We need to awaken ourselves to the need to transform the way power is shared in all aspects of society - political, economic, and intellectual. Political power is a tool for interacting and defining reality in society. It - political power - functions by virtue of collective agreement - it is not something that exists by itself. As a tool, political power is no more useful or functional than the person wielding it. It's like a hammer and chisel in the hands of someone who can make a beautiful sculpture. Political power and a hammer have potential to affect reality; they don't by themselves create reality. There is a big difference between potential and manifested reality. The key is in understanding that

human interaction is what makes each possible. If we can view politics as just another tool, it becomes less intimidating and more acceptable. If we understand that political power is a tool that must be made to serve us, we put ourselves in a better position to become masters of the tool. Political power like a simple chisel is a tool that takes a lifetime to master. It is a tool that we must begin to master so that it can serve us – not enslave us.

The vote - the mission

Exercising our right to vote is the best vehicle for creating change for women. In a democratic society, with more or less freedom of the press, the biggest influence on political tides is the vote. Votes can create an avalanche or a desert. It does not take a math whiz to figure out that women are the majority of voters, and if women chose to take power politically, it could happen overnight!

Therefore, we need to instill a sense of urgency and mission in those who are capable of supporting or leading this transformation. A sense of responsibility must accompany the will to vote. Over the last 150 years or so, the modern feminist movement has been gathering steam and is now ready to exercise political control. The world is waiting for the United States to place women in the full equation of power, not just as figureheads, but in at least 50% of all political positions, including head of state. It has already happened in the world's most advanced democracies, Sweden and Denmark. The main political parties in those countries have platforms saying that at least 40%, but not more than 60% of political positions should be held by women. We must push the Republican and Democratic parties in the United States to adopt similar platforms.

A logical question arises here: Why have women not taken power when they received the vote long ago? The

answer is not simple or always clear. Change is not an easy thing. Consider what it took for Columbus to voyage across the Atlantic in search of a new world and the work and capital invested in reaching the moon. They were gut-wrenching and vexing experiences. Women's voyage towards equality may be even more difficult, but it is our destiny and responsibility to achieve a new world.

Shared power is really the only issue that should concern WouldArt. WouldArt is involved in the feminist movement, but our concern is singular. All the other feminist issues (abortion, pay equity, equal rights, etc.) are a function of power. If men and women share power, we automatically share our decisions. This means that the mechanics of power is the issue, not the decisions made by the power structure. Equal participation of men and women in decision-making processes is paramount if the world is to change. When women become full partners in society; when gender equality is real, what is determined will ebb and flow. We will be glad to let the chips fall where they may. WouldArt has one issue – gender equality.

This analysis does not intend to imply that women are weak and dis-empowered and men are strong and empowered. However, certain generalities will be made about both men and women, bearing in mind that there are always exceptions. For example, men are more prone to physical violence than women, and women are less likely to engage in indiscriminate sex than men. These descriptions are generally true for our society, but they are not absolute. Generalities will be made for the sake of analysis; proof positive is not always possible. I want to create a logical train of ideas on the reasons why women should be empowered and in the process stimulate us all to thought and action. I do not plan on setting down indisputable principles of human behavior, merely hypotheses that encourage thinking and momentum. Further, it is not the intention of this inquiry to suggest that men and women are equal in a functional sense and should therefore share power predicated on an analysis of the capabilities of either of them.

Profound biological and psychological differences exist between men and women. Both genetics and culture have created different abilities and capacities in the sexes. In many instances, these differences have been used to disempower everybody. Sometimes it is the differences rather than the similarities that, when combined, make humankind stronger and more viable. Men and women are different and that is a good thing. Understanding that we are a community on this planet and that existence itself is tenuous makes it imperative for us to correct the imbalances that cause instability and threaten our survival. The message is clear; the writing is on the wall. If we don't become a more cohesive community on this planet, the consequences can be disastrous. This book is not an apocalyptic vision, but the potential for disaster is real, and dire consequences should motivate us toward corrective action.

Change - liberation – presumption - continuum

Women and men must change the way they see themselves and each other. We are basically what we are – good – bad – and indifferent. What is required is not changing what we are, but how we relate to one another and ourselves. This is the heart of our transformation. In recognizing and utilizing each other's strengths and weaknesses, we transform our interactions and add to our individual being-ness. We don't lose any qualities of manhood or womanhood; we simply create new or expanded dimensions. Changing the way we relate personally happens simultaneously with change in the institutions that regulate our interactions.

The forthcoming critiques of the institutions of government, business, religion and marriage are made in a constructive spirit. The goal is to transform these institutions, not eliminate them. The intention is to reveal their weaknesses so they can become stronger and stable. As a result our communities will become more viable.

The overall effort of this work is to contribute to the liberation of both men and women. When women's position in society is altered; so is men's position. Clearly we will either rise or fall together. To use an analogy, we are building a home here on Earth, and we have made a decision not to utilize all of our resources — primarily women - to the fullest. It is like a carpenter dividing her tools and materials and saying, "I am not going to use half the tools in my box or a substantial amount of the lumber and nails in my possession." Another analogy is playing chess and refusing to move certain pieces. Not advantageously using certain players because of a lack of knowledge is one thing, but refusing to use them out of selfishness or perceived dominance is something else all together. Neglecting to use the queen in chess hurts one's game badly and is not a very smart strategy. Women are our chess queens, and they are powerful allies.

A friend said it was presumptuous of me to write a feminist paper because I am not a woman. Is it presumptuous to want to free myself from oppressing and being oppressed by women? Doesn't it make sense to help free women and create a world in which there is greater harmony, productivity and viability for the future? By attempting to understand women better, I gain knowledge about women, men and the world. I want to deepen my quest in life and embrace my own experience today, to be better than yesterday.

Supposedly the wisest words ever written are "Know thyself." Self-knowledge is obtained in many different ways; for men, one of the best seats in the house is the perspective view through female eyes. I see women as part of me, as helping to define and enhance myself. Wanting to understand my own weakness is a great part of my

motivation to become a stronger man. Men, by making the effort to understand women have a view in a window into themselves.

I see women as an integral part of my world. They help to define and enhance my life. Women hold the key to male strength and knowledge just as men hold that key for women. By helping women grow stronger, I help myself grow stronger. That obvious truth is based on a simple equation: if I make you stronger, you will in turn empower me. "I'll scratch your back if you'll scratch mine." Basic self interest is part of my motivation to help women grow stronger.

Another of my motivations is my desire to create an environment of equality and better opportunity for my daughters. I want a better world for my girls than the one I grew up in. I would like them to have more options than are currently available. My mother worked as an executive secretary for over twenty years and related many examples of discrimination. My four sisters have never had as many options in school, sports, recreation and employment as I have. It would be better for all of us if we were all dealt cards from the same deck.

This is a feminist analysis from the male perspective, with the intention of aiding all. This is one man's point of view, not the only point of view. It is but a note in a chorus of commentary about men and women and their interactions. Male perspectives are important to the feminist movement for a number of reasons. If women excluded or limited men's participation, they would be doing the same thing that men have done to them over the last five millennia. Male domination has brought an imbalance to the world and created an illusion of stability based upon force and the threat of force. True community is built upon trust and mutual benefit. We don't have trust in our institutions today. Rarely are things done for the benefit of all.

Men and women are mentors to one another. Each is stronger when we trust and rely on the other, but in large part we have failed to support one another. Women will not share power in this world without the agreement and understanding of men. Men will not have a world worth two cents without the cooperation and involvement of women. It is time for all of us to realize that we need and must nurture one another. Life is not a competition between the sexes; it is a continuum!

A structural transformation in the way power is shared must be accomplished in an enduring way. The job at hand is not just convincing women that they must assume power, but educating men to its necessity as well. The question is not whether we will change, but how we will change. All social transformations take time to digest. Women can assume power overnight, but understanding and acceptance might take a little longer. We are on a long journey (we all hope) in the human quest. We must take provisions and precautions for our trip, make the right plans and double-check our list of priorities.

Each one of us has an influence on the political climate of the day, and today's climate affects tomorrow's history. No matter what one believes or professes, it counts. Even a small influence can be very significant. If your point of view can change someone's mind even a little, that person might change the world! It's as if we were cooking up a big stew. Each one of us adds an ingredient. Some of us add a lot of spice, so we add a distinct flavor to the pot. Some add the meat, and others the vegetables. The lesson for all of us is to be aware of what we are adding to the stew.

There is a profound difference between those who see themselves as influential and those who do not. I do not have statistics to substantiate the claim of the effectiveness of people who feel powerful, but I know that when I feel powerful, I am. The opposite is also true. If we want to empower women, we need to influence the way they see themselves.

Responsibility – hunch - I to eye

When we take individual responsibility for our own ideas; our influence increases dramatically. Knowing that one has influence increases one's motivation, and that motivation drives us to clarify our position. Better understanding helps one to be more effective. Clear, organized thoughts strengthen the message. Religious evangelists, politicians, and business leaders understand this circular reasoning very well and make good use of it. The job of WouldArt is to promote a clear agenda that will truly advance civilization. This clear agenda is something that people want to buy into because they need to have it. We are charged with creating a strong rationale for women to share power - one that makes sense and is clear, concise, and persuasive.

My intention is to stimulate more dialogue on the subject of women and men and the power they don't share. If my only accomplishment is to provoke you to think about this topic, then I have succeeded. I challenge all people to articulate their own critique or defense of the status quo. Dynamic and vigorous thought is the lifeblood of the human experience. We need fresh thoughts as much as we need fresh air.

The Greek philosopher Democritus said that "all that exists is atoms and empty space; everything else is opinion". The comedian Lily Tomlin said "Reality is nothing more than a collective hunch". This is my "opinion" about an aspect of the "hunch." I don't want my descendants to look back and think I did little or nothing to steer the course of the human ship in a positive way. We all have a responsibility to make a mighty effort to bring about a better world.

Until we express ourselves to others and get their feedback, we don't really know what our ideas will spark. In this essay I shall do my best to express my ideas about gender, our planet and myself. This is not a treatise of facts although there are many facts in this work. This is a book of my opinions that I hope will spark your thinking.

Let me tell a story about young man I know. The story makes some good points about change and the ability to change. This young man was not a child prodigy and did not do well in public school. He was not stupid, just not motivated in academic directions. He was more interested in having a good time than doing "academic" stuff. He would cut classes or cutup in school at the drop of a hat. He was a goodtime Charlie, a good old boy. He was always ready to have fun and stir the pot.

From an early age he was motivated to make money. He had several jobs before he started working regularly as a carpenter at age 13. He worked because he came from a large family with modest means. He needed to work for the "extras" in life and to help his family. He was a hard worker and was very focused on carpentry. He learned to build houses, and he helped build a lot of them over the eight years he worked for a local builder.

The story of this young man up to this point is not unusual except for the fact while in the last grade in high school he decided he wanted to go to college. His academic record was, shall we be kind and say, very modest. He was moved from grade to grade, promoted each year, with poor marks in most of his subjects. He got average grades in art, choir, wood shop and metal shop, but he did not do well at all in his academic classes (the 3 R's). He had terrible reading and writing skills, and his math skills had not risen above those in basic arithmetic.

When the young man announced he wanted to go to college, his friends laughed at him; his parents told him to think about carpentry. He asked the high school guidance counselor if he could have a letter of recommendation to present to perspective colleges and the answer was – No! He was told he was not college material. His reading, writing and math skills were less than those of an average eighth grader. However, he had a vision for himself and was motivated. As a senior in high school he read his first book *The Carpetbaggers* by Harold Robbins, and decided he wanted more.

Why this boy was motivated to begin his academic career and go to college is the real point of this story. He wanted to transform his own life. He said to himself "I can change; I can learn; I can grow". He had two allies: an uncle, who was also his dentist, and a brother-in-law. They supported his efforts and encouraged him to apply to college. He applied to thirty-two schools; all of them turned him down except one, Mayville State College. He left home for the first time and went out-of-state to Mayville, North Dakota. He found sympathetic people to help him overcome his deficiencies and little by little he became a scholar. He had the right motivation; in class he was not concerned with a grade, but rather with what he could learn. He discovered the joy of learning for its own sake. He overcame his deficiencies and went on to complete a BS degree in psychology. The point of this story is that people can change no matter how extraordinary the odds are against them.

How do we modify a society, a culture, or a species? The answer is by changing the way we think. We cannot afford to continue excluding more than half of the world's population - women.

How can you move a mountain? You can move a mountain by moving one spoonful of dirt at a time. Women should not be left out of the solution or the process. Working together the focus would not be on how long it would take to move a mountain, but rather which mountain do we want to move and where do we want to use the dirt?

The young man whose story I related had a mountain of ignorance in his head. He needed to remove the ignorance and replace it with a mountain of knowledge. His story is about attitude and having a sense of mission or purpose. He had confidence in himself even though the road ahead seemed impossible. He had a place to go, a goal to strive for, and new horizons to look forward to. We all need new horizons to gaze at and strive towards. We all need goals. Working together we can reach new horizons. The important thing is to have goals in our lives.

    We are new to this planet and new to ourselves. This planet is a wonderful place in which to live. By working together we can make it the garden it once was and deserves to be again. By we, I mean men and women. It is a matter of attitude and intention and hard work. The essence of life is in the mind's eye: if we can see **I to eye** we can move mountains and the world. Let's get to work and move mountains!

Chapter two

The Order of Things

Classes – Hierarchies - Pecking Order

Karl Marx begins his classic work <u>The Communist Manifesto</u> with the sentence, "The history of all hitherto existing society is the history of class struggles." Marx saw the struggle between rich and poor and the unequal distribution of goods and services as a systemic problem in the world of his time. To a great extent he was right, both then and now. The world still has a fundamental problem with the distribution of goods and services, and class struggle is an ongoing problem. One of the main principles associated with Marx's explanation for poverty and exploitation is economic determinism. Economic determinism posits that people are ruled beyond their control by the financial forces that surround them. Marx asserts that economic forces and divisions of labor produce classes in society. Those who are at the top of the economic pyramid exploit those below, and this in turn creates struggle between classes.

There is a lot of truth in Marx's analysis, but some classes are formed before economics enters the picture. Not all class struggle is based on economics. The economic pyramid is a hierarchy that is superimposed upon an already-established class structure. While it is true that economics defines and creates classes in society, more primal forces determine human classes such as race and ethnicity. Nature creates the classes, not economics. Humans categorize everything and create classes and establish the hierarchies within and between them. We establish categories based on sex, intellect, age, attractiveness, survivability, strengths and abilities.

The most defining division between any species biologically is by sex. The largest and oldest struggle is between the biggest groups of people - men and women. They are the point and counterpoint in an ongoing polemic – the big class struggle. It has many manifestations:

psychological; spiritual, sexual, economic, social, legal, etc. Men and women hinder and propel one another. Since we are different, we provoke one another in both thought and action. Women are the numerically larger of the classes for two reasons: war and biology. Men are the strongest for the same reasons.

The synthesis of the sexes on a psychological level is cooperation, companionship, community and continuity. On a physical level the synthesis is children. Sexual love is a real and compelling physical synthesis of men and women. Children are the byproduct of this union and ensure the continuation of the species. People are more powerful together than apart. We provide a difference or contrast for one another and the result, if we utilize the juxtaposition, is a more refined and powerful synthesis. However, for the most part we don't utilize our opposing strengths. Women are denied equal decision-making power in the world today. By denying women equal input in making decisions; we are not fully utilizing their strengths and capabilities. As a result humankind suffers from the consequences.

Most animal species establish hierarchies. Wolves, chimpanzees and chickens establish pecking orders to insure that only the strongest survive and give cohesion to their family groups. The chances of survival are better in a cohesive group. Structure helps a group to survive. Humans are no different in their instinct to survive and be cohesive, and we too establish pecking orders.

Establishing pecking orders is not inherently bad; it serves a useful and necessary function. Establishing pecking orders is a refining process of life through which a species is made stronger and more adaptable to changing environments. However, creating new classes or new powers within a class often disturbs the status quo. Disturbing the status quo is not necessarily a bad thing if it assists needed growth. Sometimes subjugation is part of the process, but excessive subjugation or persecution disturbs

the process of growth and adaptation by causing conflict and disruption.

Humans display a characteristic propensity to dominate the less strong of the species, in many instances to the point of abuse. Oppression occurs even when it is detrimental to all parties. Gradations of oppression range from calling someone a derogatory name to genocide and slavery. In the animal kingdom domination exists, but usually not oppression. The persecution of the weaker in the human species is an unnecessary limitation and tax upon both the weak and the strong. Humanity runs into trouble when different classes or strata within a class fight with one another to the point of annihilation.

Family - Mother Love - mystical force - original family

When does domination and conflict become oppression? What is the purpose of oppression? Let's first examine how hierarchies and classes are formed, and then consider how oppression occurs. The struggle between classes starts at the smallest unit of community, the family. The family is (Assumption – 337.2) two or more people who bond together and proceed through life as a unit. A man and woman is not, contrary to popular assumption, the primary family unit. The mother and child is the primary family unit. No other human relationship is as fundamental or indispensable as the mother and child. All that is necessary to perpetuate the species is a male acquaintance and the mother/child bond. Think about humans millions of years ago. People were unaware that sex was related to reproduction. The early "caveman" probably did not know he was a father any more than a rabbit does. The real family in the Stone Age was the mother and the baby. People of a million years ago grouped together for protection, hunting, and sex, but most of all because of the mother/child bond. The family as we know it today did not exist. Monogamist

relationships among our ancient relatives are speculative at best. We have a hard time maintaining monogamy today, but a million years ago fidelity was not necessarily a big concern or issue.

Although a man, woman and child is the traditional conception of a family. A mother and child really is the first family unit; the building block and the sociological base for human communities and groups.

Women have babies because of biological and psychological compulsions. The biological driving force is hormones; the psychological reason women want babies is love and affiliation. Does a mother need a child in order to survive? The answer is no; therefore, there must be other reasons that women want babies. It certainly isn't because they are easy to have and take care of. Women intrinsically understand the psychological and spiritual value of the mother/child bond and the benefits of the sacrifices it engenders. Something extremely powerful pushes women to want to be mothers. Biology alone is not enough of a compulsion or explanation why women want babies. There is a mystical force which compels women to want babies. This mystical force of creation, is love, and is created from and centered in the mother/child bond.

How love got here initially is a "first cause" issue; like the big bang theory. No one can say or answer why love exists, but no one can deny that love does exists. In the same regard, there is no question that love comes from a mother. The mother/child bond is crucial and essential for all of civilization. Basic social relationships are possible because the mother/child bond exists. Why does a mother love her child? Because it comes from her, is first part of her; the child is first and foremost the mother! A mother loves a child because she loves herself. A mother loves herself because her mother loved her.

Love is the raison d'etre for cohesive human existence, progression and possibility. Women understand love in a way that men cannot and do not. Giving birth to a child also gives birth to love. The mystic force of love comes from the equation that was set in motion – a mother and child. Love is the glue, which binds a mother to her child, and it is the major reason that communities can form, function and stay together. If a child does not learn love from someone early on, it will not be able to appreciate the many social principles which are necessary to hold a community together: trust, cooperation, shared sacrifice, and so on.

Mother love is the basis of all love – even self love. Everything we know about love is derived from mother love. If a child does not get mother love or some facsimile of it, the child fails to thrive. Everything we value, as humans, is dependent upon love. Love is the soil in which all human characteristics and experience grow. If the soil is not tended and cultivated properly, growth is restricted. Love defines value. Love permits value to form and function.

Mother love teaches the principle of shared sacrifice for the common good. Mother love filters the mind's eye of humanity. It accepts diversity and divergence and holds people together for its own sake. This is a very important point – love is its own reward.

Community exists because the individual members understand the value of human bonding. Our first bond is with our mothers before we are even born. The associations and community that we form are not possible without mother love. All institutions in civilization are an addendum to the mother/child bond. Cohesiveness of culture and civilization comes from mother love. Nothing in human experience is more sacred or profound. Any inclination we have (Assumption 337.8) as a species to cooperate, progress and dream is derived from the mother/child bond. It teaches mutual sharing, sacrifice and dependency. Everything that we have and value, now, in civilization is derived from mother love.

A man and a woman can learn to love one another because they have first learned the idea of love from their respective mothers or mother figures. Many studies have shown that without adequate mothering a child or animal will grow up incapable of socializing with others.

The traditional conception of family (mother, father and child) of today is derived from the original family – mother and child. The original and traditional family leads to communities. Without the presence of the family, the community would have no basis for existence. Community is possible because it has its roots in the family, and all family is derived from the first family - mother and child.

Oppression

Because a mother has fears for the survival of both herself and her child, she is compelled to certain defensive actions. In order to defend and protect a child, she must insist that her child obey her commands. The child listens and submits to mother's greater wisdom, experience, and, if necessary, force. The Mother is dominant, and the child is dependent. That establishes the first rule of primal human hierarchy. This class relationship is not, normally, abusive. Mothers dominate their children in order to protect and enhance them.

Husbands and wives are not normally abusive of one another. Abusing someone is a learned behavior. The driving forces are usually fear and hate. Fear is one of the most powerful forces propelling human behavior. People fear not receiving gratification, or they fear the consequences of a particular behavior; they fear deprivation, or rejection, or any number of human anxieties. Fear-based reactions can manifest in the inappropriate behavior we call oppression. The pattern of oppression is learned in the interaction between males and females, in the family nest when goals and expectations are not being met.

Lack of food, clothing, shelter, and sex are some of the prime causes for anxiety, fear, hatred, and the resulting behavior - oppression. We fear subjugation or loss of stature, so we act in an aggressive or defensive way to forestall domination and diminishment. If our goals and expectations are not met, we get angry and retaliate. We want what we want, and if we can't coerce, cajole, or concoct a way of getting "ours," we resort to more forceful and devious means. Retaliation can be covert or overt, passive or aggressive, and sometimes very subtle. When our retaliation is out of proportion to the unfulfilled expectation - abuse or oppression follows. We learn retaliation behavior in our families from our parents and siblings at a very early age. We observe our mothers, fathers and siblings first, and then from interaction with our peers and mates we learn the finer points of oppression. Everyone participates in oppression with someone at some time

This is not to say that human nature is cruel. People get frustrated and don't know how or don't take the time to learn how to react in a kind and appropriate manner. Everybody agrees with the golden rule – treat people how you like to be treated, but we all know it is easier said than done. Oppression in its minor forms is inappropriate behavior, but not cruel and malicious. It usually takes an abnormal amount of deficiencies, circumstance or conditioning to make someone really cruel. However, small amounts of abuse do come rather easily, and in many instances they are not readily noticeable to even the people involved.

Oppression can be so institutionalized that we don't notice it or its consequences. Gender oppression is institutionalized in our world today. Many people are unaware of the extent of gender oppression. All of us participate in some kind of oppression in one form or another. Many patterns of abuse are stereotyped according to gender. Sex roles and scripts for gender oppression vary somewhat from culture to culture and over time. How we relate to one another is a complex amalgam of what we are continuously learning from our individual and group interactions.

The younger the person, the more susceptible they are to pressure. Young people are pressured to conform to society, peer and family thinking patterns. Social behavior is interactive. Our individual behavior adds to the equation of influences that make up the gender scripts we live by. For those of us who have children, it is easy to understand that young people have a profound effect on their parents. Having children produces a revolution in our social actions and philosophical thinking. Children are a major life correction. Parents think of life as BC (before children) and AD (after diapers). We define one another and refine ourselves continually throughout life. One doesn't get the same script or thinking pattern and play it endlessly.

Life is a continuum of give and take. Our behavior is framed; to a great extent by the gender behavior patterns we are taught. We learn behavior sequences and patterns first in our families – from our parents, sisters and brothers. Besides the biological influences we have a social dynamic that forms a person's gender perspective. The family is where we learn how to be male or female. We learn the nuts and bolts of being a boy or girl in our family dens. The family is not isolated from the community and vice versa. The family is the wellspring from which all communities flow.

Gender oppression, which we first learn and practice in our families, is then superimposed on the institutions we construct to regulate our communities. The components of gender oppression become a pattern for relations in larger groups. Institutions in turn influence the family that spawns it. An institution is defined as any group, either formal or informal, that binds people and resources together for mutual benefit, such as for religious, business, military, or governmental purposes.

Consciousness – Insecurity – Eternal Questions

The root of oppression is not economic, but psychological and spiritual. Marx's compatriot Engel's wrote: <u>The materialist conception of history starts from the proposition that the production of the means to support human life and, next to production, the exchange of things produced, is the basis of all social structure; that in every society that has appeared in history, the manner in which wealth is distributed and society divided into classes or orders is dependent upon what is produced, how it is produced, and how the products are exchanged. From this point of view, the final causes of all social changes and political revolutions are to be sought, not in men's brains, not in men's better insights into eternal truth and justice, but in changes in the modes of production and exchange.</u>

We have to look deeper into the human condition to understand the basis of our social structure. We must understand that before there is a mode of production and exchange; there is a deficit, a need – a wanting. Before there is an action to eat, clothe or shelter ourselves, a thought is manifested in consciousness. This thought or need is a base psychological state related to a deprivation. A psychological deprivation asks for a solution. It is in the formulation of the solution that the relationship between people produces the mechanics of oppression. If I want food and there is not even enough for one person, would I be inclined to share it with a wife and three children? Perhaps if I were well-fed the day before, but what if I've been hungry for a month? If I were the man of the family and physically stronger than my mate and children, I might take the food by force if necessary. If I were one of the children, I might take the food by stealth. The point is that under severe deprivation any person is capable of oppression. Circumstances do not have to be severe for oppressive behavior to manifest itself, and oppression itself can be very mild or subtle.

Descartes' axiom, "I think therefore I am," highlights one of the primary dilemmas of humankind, which is insecurity. The statement yearns to assert: "I exist – I think – and I am insecure about it". Or vice versa, "I am insecure because I think". Either way it speaks about the vulnerability of human identity and thinking. Our very capacity for thought and consciousness involves inherent qualities of insecurity about what we think and who we are. Humans feel insecure because we think. Our thoughts drive our insecurity and subsequent behavior. When we feel insecure about something necessary like food, we think about solving that particular problem.

Necessity is the mother of invention, and also the father of insecurity. We invent things in order to address our necessities and allay our insecurities. Insecurity is built into human thought, and it can cause behavior that is less than noble. The more we understand this fact, the better equipped we are to manage ourselves.

The fundamental human question of concern is not "How will we survive?" but "Why should we live?" Animals are only concerned with the question of how to survive. Humans have a greater capacity to think and therefore to ask, "Why should we live?" The "how" question is concerned with the mechanics of survival. The question of "why" is concerned with the quality of existence. Because we ask the question about the mechanics of why we live, spirituality becomes one of the most fundamental aspects of consciousness.

Why we live frames how we live. When we come to terms with the reasons for why we should live, we can construct a methodology of how we can survive. It is of vital importance not to confuse the order of this analysis. Putting the survival question of "how to live" before the inquiry of "why" is like sailing a ship without a rudder, or trying to build a house without a blueprint. Much of the Earth's most serious problems are related to a lack of planning and

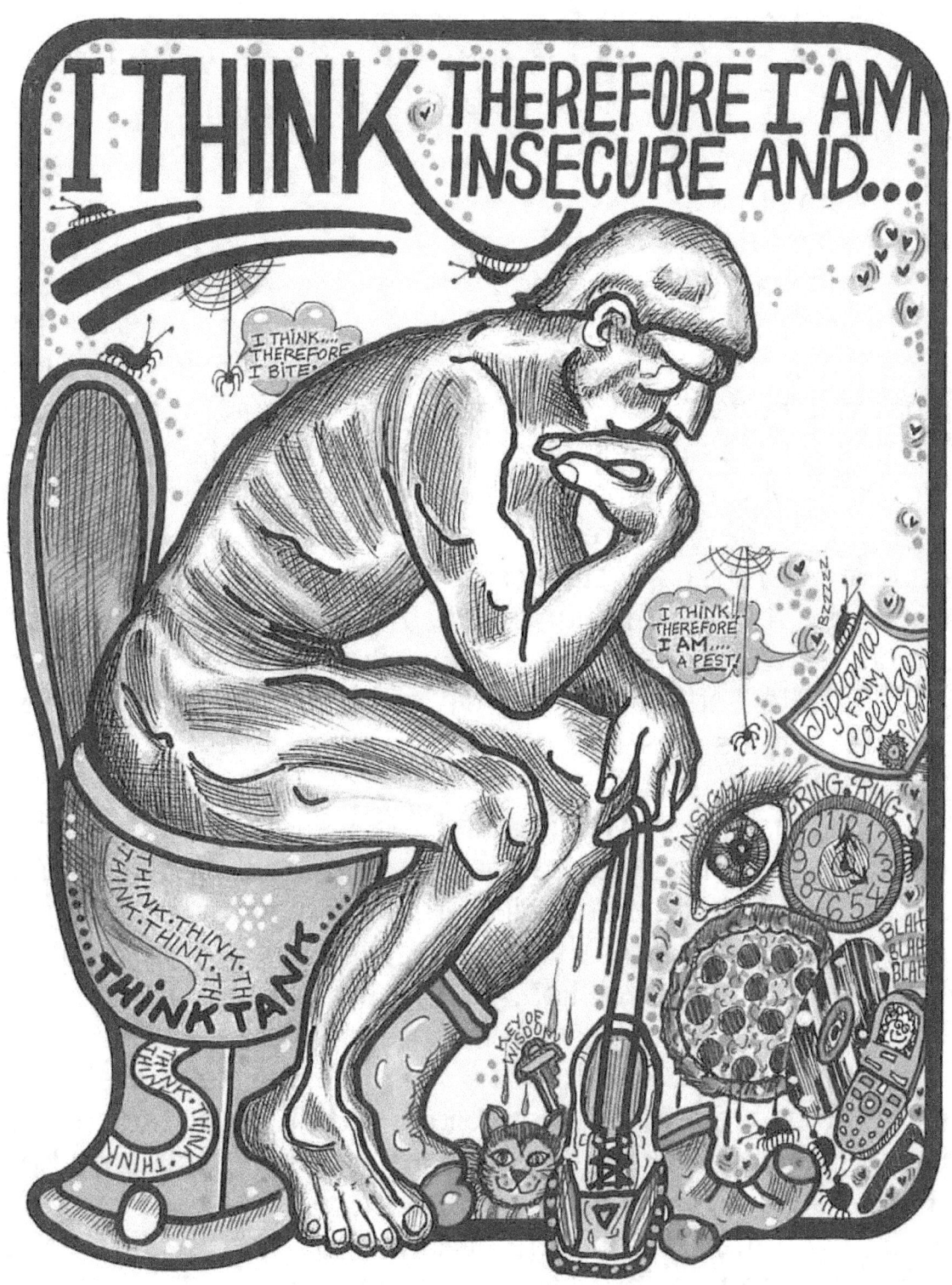

intention. In other words humans answer many of their needs/necessities by asking 'how' first, instead of 'why'. That is a mistake.

What are the most important questions we address in our lives? They are the three eternal questions:

1. Who are we?
2. Where did we come from?
3. And where are we going?

We ask these questions because we want to establish what is important. We also ask them because we can, and we answer these questions to establish the rationale for the 'how and why' of human behavior. These questions live with us from the day we are born to the day we die. Do they get answered? Hindus, Catholics and Buddhist all have different answers. This is a matter of much debate and controversy, which we will address later in this discourse. For now, it is important to understand that we are motivated and pushed by these questions to certain behaviors, whether we like them or not.

The how and why of our lives is driven by the three eternal questions. We have gotten to a stage in human history in which it becomes imperative that we guide our own evolution more carefully. Our volition has always been involved in our evolution, but now we must use this knowledge in a more dynamic and calculated process. We must guide our own evolution more deliberately. We must drive human evolution, not follow it. If we can seize this principle - of the order of questions - "Why?" first and then "How?" - we humans will evolve more rapidly. If we don't do it soon, we may destroy the quality of life that is left on this Earth, and perhaps our very existence.

Life really is a puzzle to be solved. The eternal questions are key pieces in the puzzle of life and the unification of the psychological and spiritual orders of

consciousness. We are part of a greater equation, encompassing all of existence. The puzzle of life is not only the design configuration but also the process. The process of solving the human puzzle is part of the puzzle.

This question of "why we live" is so important that spirituality becomes axiomatic in the formulation of our basic thoughts, relationships, and institutions. One of the first (assumption 338.3) institutions created was religion. Religion was needed in order to deal with the tremendous insecurities and mysteries faced by early humans – the three eternal questions. It laid the foundation for other institutions to follow. In fact religion continues to play the dominant role in the formulation of the basic institutions of business, government, and social structure. The reason is because we are still dealing with primal insecurity - the three eternal questions - and we always will.

Estrus – Menstruation – Thinking – Pleasure Principle

We must ask ourselves the question of how consciousness came into being. Did humans a million years ago have consciousness of themselves? Perhaps. Did humans think about themselves five millions of years ago? At some time in the ancient history of humans or humanoid primates, we did not possess a large degree of self-awareness or consciousness. We did not arrive on the human scene fully conscious – we evolved. (assumption 338.387) This being the case, what were the factors which enabled humans to become self-aware in an analytical way which distinguishes us from all other animals? We have to think back, way back, before humans knew how to make a fire or use a club as a tool. What made us self-aware and how did we begin to think?

The answer to these questions is not easily obtained, and probably most thinking on this subject is conjecture. However, there are certain clues, which support a thesis that

consciousness in humans is derived from women's biology; and more specifically female sexuality. In terms of reproduction, human females are different from most other mammals because they do not go into heat; they have a menstrual cycle rather than an estrus cycle. Non-human animals have sex when the female is biologically ready, and the purpose of sex is reproduction. The sexual behavior is a compulsion, and these animals have little choice. Most animals have an instinctual drive to mate, which is related more to pheromones and rhythmic cycles than with a pleasure principle. In contrast, humans have sex whenever they want, and it doesn't necessarily have anything to do with reproduction.

Animals enjoy sex too, but human sex is based more on a pleasure principle than on a biological urge. Animals are driven by pheromones and biological urges which they have no control over. Although pheromones and biological urge are part of the human equation, the physical and psychological compulsions are the dominant motivations for human sexual activity. We choose the time, place and person we have sex with – animals don't have as much discretion. Parts of the human genitals seem to be designed solely for pleasure in both male and female. These "parts" don't have any biological function other than giving pleasure.

It seems logical that a mechanism for the development of human consciousness is related to human biological freedom to engage in sex at ones own discretion. Thinking about the pleasurable process of sex activity is what brought about the stimulation for human consciousness. Therefore, the pleasure principle of sex thinking, is the engine of motivation for the development of consciousness. The key factor in this thesis is female biology. Early woman, for whatever reason, was not tied to a mating cycle (estrus), she menstruated. Menstruation freed woman from the autopilot compulsion to procreate. Woman's anatomy allowed her to enjoy the process of mating; she began to think of ways to repeat the pleasurable circumstance of sex. The operative word in the last sentence is "think"; she began to think!

Both men and women have a sex drive, but it is women who have always acted as gatekeepers to sexuality. Women are gatekeepers to sexual activity now, and they were five millions years ago too. Women brought about the possibility of thinking of sex and its pleasure as a function of their menstrual cycle. Because women are capable of sex at any time of their choosing, they are in the best position to do the choosing. It is women who initiate the platform of sexual pleasure because they have a menstrual cycle that allows them choice. I am not talking about the sex act, rather the capability of sex as a pleasurable activity – an idea. By "capability of sex" I mean more of a conceptual possibility than a physical reality. Because of the menstrual cycle women create the possibility of sex as a pleasurable thought. This is a concept. An idea! It still is a very good idea! The menstrual cycle freed us from the rhythmic time clock of mating. It gave us the capability to think about sex and when we could have it.

In another sense, the menstrual cycle connects us to time. Because we could have sex at anytime of our choosing, we thought about time. Thoughts of sex activity initiate time as a destination. Sex and menstruation creates a time awareness. We think about sex because it is available and pleasurable. Thinking about something you want is pleasurable - a pleasure principle. Sex as a distant activity involves planning, calculation and delayed gratification. The pleasure principle is a byproduct of the menstrual cycle. Thinking is a byproduct of the pleasure principle. The possibility of sex at a time of choosing initiates thinking. Time as a concept is a byproduct of thinking about the pleasure of obtaining sex later. In addition, menstruation is part of the biological clock that generates thoughts of time. Because the female is menstruating regularly, she is a walking clock. The gatekeeper of sex is a thinking person and therefore in a

position of leadership in the development of human consciousness and motivation. The sex gatekeeper is also the time keeper and the initiator of thinking.

Early man played his part in the development of consciousness, but if it were not for women's liberating menstrual cycle, men would only have sex at cyclical intervals, like cats and dogs. The sex process for humans would have been more mechanical if not for menstruation. The limitation of the estrus cycle has been significant in keeping other mammalian animals at a lower stage of conscious awareness and hence mental development.

Sex, of course, wasn't the only factor which leads to human awareness, but the menstrual cycle is of paramount importance in the stimulation that allowed the human brain to grow and develop. It seems fair to state (Assumption 341.8) that, with an estrus cycle of sex, humans probably wouldn't have risen far above other animals. Although there is no way of determining the stage in human evolution the menstrual cycle developed. The menstrual cycle probably preceded the increased cranial capacity of early humans. Menstruation was a prime reason that human brains evolved. There was a convergence in evolution of the menstrual cycle, coupled with the pleasure principle that motivated humans to think. Like everything in evolution – it took a long time. Human brains grew because of the increased demand for sexual pleasure. Our brains are still evolving – and we still crave sex.

Women were at the leading edge of human evolution because their biological design disposed them to think; creativity is the result. Biology favored women as the keepers of the flame, the spark of the human intellect. Women's leadership in the development of consciousness produced the first societies and communities. The first human communities were matrifocal. Most Old and New Stone Age, Copper Age, and early Bronze Age societies, until about 2500 B.C.E., were matrifocal. One has only to take a casual look at the physical world to see that its overwhelming principle is feminine. Mother Nature really is feminine in operation. The cyclical seasons; birth and decay and the rebirth of both plants and animals are a female dominated process.

This analysis does not negate the fact that the male of the human species, of all species, had a large part to play with the development and progression of a species. However, the burden of survival rests more heavily on female than male animals. We could still exist if males were out numbered a hundred to one. What would the world be like if there was only one female to every hundred males? The burden of consciousness and civilization rests more heavily on female than male humans. Early man followed the lead of woman, who provided man more opportunity for sex and pleasure than his counterpart in the animal kingdom. Sex acted as a positive reinforcement and motivator on early humans (not to mention modern people) to learn, grow and adapt.

The female has always understood and appreciated the partnership of males in sexual pleasure. For women, sex is a pleasurable exchange for dealing with men. Women have men as their sex pleasure partners. This is a very important consideration because the sex partnership is one of the fundamental parts of community. It is the basis for the initial relationship between adults of the opposite sex. Community flows from a common interest, a shared goal or desire. Collaborative thinking and behavior is the result of this partnership.

Male domination

Male domination of power and politics in the last 4500 years is unfortunate. For one half of a partnership to overshadow its mate is not a good equation. A logical partnership exists between men and women, but women's role in this partnership has been subordinated. Women have been stripped of their natural leadership. Women's absence from the decision-making loop is so institutionalized and it has happened for so long and is so pervasive - that we only recently have taken notice of it. It is vitally important for us to realize that together men and women are a team rather than opposing sides. The destiny of humans is like ship in a mighty river with many tributaries that flows into an ocean. We are stuck in a minor tributary and in danger of grounding our ship before we reach the main river. The possibilities for our future are extraordinary if we can stop abusing one another and put that energy towards something productive.

    The question naturally arises as to how men came to a position of domination over women. It wasn't always this way, or was it? There isn't a clear-cut answer to this question. History is a half-told story at best, and many times (Assumption 343.97) is either forgotten or fabricated. However, there are many clues, bits and pieces of art, artifact and written evidence we can use to understand the past. A case can be made that male domination emerged from man's superior physical strength. Early humans (not to mention modern humans) relied on physical force as a means of communication and persuasion. It is not hard for us to imagine a cave-dwelling family being hungry or starving. If food is scarce, who is going to get the little bit that comes in? The fact that man has physical superiority puts him in possession of an ability he can choose to exercise; the male can take the food if he chooses. Why does man use physical force? Answer - because he can.

    Men use physical force to dominate others because it works. This is not to say that males are naturally disposed to being violent. A male is born of and nurtured by a mother, who gives him love and affection. Mothers don't teach their sons to be cruel and violent; one has to learn it from another source.

As a man grows away from his mother and associates with other boys and men, he becomes aware of his physical prowess. If the right set of circumstances happens and a man is aware of his superior physical ability, he is capable of using force. A woman is too, but she is surrounded by males, most of whom are stronger than she is. Therefore, she tends not to want to engage others on a physical basis. More significantly, women are the vessel of life, nurturing and love. Women are keepers of the sexual force – the soft force. Men and women are not different in their motivation for violence and warfare. Women are capable of killing too. The difference lies in the reasons each has for propagation and defense. Men are more willing to engage and propagate violence because they are good at it, and they can. Women can be violent too, but a woman's violence tends to be defensive. The force women use is more reasoned, subtle and calculated. Women use the soft force because they know they cannot win with direct force in relation to men. Women employ the soft force because they are required to protect and nurture their young.

Hunger, anger, fear, sorrow, and hostility are some of the circumstances that can elicit physical force. Most instances of violence, however, don't occur when the conditions are life threatening or extreme. Violence and domination happen much more as a function of appetite rather than deprivation. Force is widely used in our society to procure things to satisfy our wants and desires. A man wants sex so he rapes someone, or he wants the tastiest treat so he pushes someone out of the way, or he wants stature so he beats up someone. You may say that most men are not this way, but look closely at almost any man, today, and you will find at least some instances of force at work. It may not always be physical force, but most men will use force in economic, social, political and intellectual situations. Men are conditioned by both biology and culture to be aggressive, and this translates to being forceful and sometimes violent.

Many times there is a subtle distinction between force and violence. Is it not violent to move your car into another lane abruptly even if the maneuver is successful? How about sending advertising email to 100,000 people? Is telling a subordinate that his bow tie looks funny an example of psychological violence? Violence is not just a slap in the face; it can be a word slap or car position slap. There are a million other examples of diminishing or denigrating another person or group without physical touching. Force is a mindset. Physical force is the grandfather of all force and establishes the equation of force as a means to an end.

What happens much more frequently than overt violence is the threat of physical aggression or some other force. Using physical stature in an intimidating way is very common. Talking in a loud and angry voice usually has the implied threat of physical violence or domination. "I'm going to take you to court and rake you over the coals" means "I am going to get you!" Violence and intimidation are effective means to an end.

We all live in our imaginations and fantasy at least part of the time each day. For men, fantasy about physical force is very common. It may involve intimidation, revenge, protection, an image of oneself as a hero or sports star, or any combination of these and other imaginings. Most men participate in a wide variety of vicarious violence, through sports, business, law, etc. In our supposedly civilized world, both actual and vicarious male violence are very real and almost universal.

In addition, many men are unaware of the presence and content of their own violent thinking. Violence is everywhere; you cannot read the newspaper or watch television without seeing it. In movies, books, sports, arcade games, in the graffiti on the walls, we see violence. We have violence in our thoughts because every sector and stratum of society conditions us. It is woven and bred into our culture. Humans all use force to get their way, but men are more prone to violence.

Women do not tend (Assumption 347.5) to as much violence as males. There are two good reasons for this: first, women are physically weaker than men and usually lose in combat. Second, females understand, via the mother/child bond, the value of cooperation as a better alternative to violence. From the male point of view, violence is a reliable method for getting what you want. In the female mind, violence is too crude a method for obtaining what one needs. The female mind understands that violence and love are opposing actions. If one wants love, don't use violence. Females know that children who are beaten into submission lack spontaneity, creativity and resourcefulness. Children who are lovingly guided are more adaptable and capable of survival.

Although there is a big difference in the methods men and women use to obtain things in life, the biggest difference is goal orientation. The male mind is more often than not win/lose oriented; the female mind is more commonly win/win. Men feel that possession of things (family, food, shelter, land, tools, etc.) is best achieved through aggression and domination of one sort or another. A woman's goal is not to own a child or family, but to live in harmony with and nurture it. The difference in goals for men and women is control vs. cooperation. Man took control because he had the physical strength to do so. Woman did not see control as advantageous or necessary. This is a very important distinction for understanding the mindset of both sexes. Our behavior in life is guided by our psychological and philosophical orientation. Men are more often than not trying to be first by making someone else second. Women want to be first too, but are more willing to share the position with someone else.

Matrifocal Societies

The most basic unit of association in nature is the mother/child. Mother/child is the foundation upon which all relationships in societies are based. From Mother/child grows the traditional family (mother, father and children), extended family (aunts, uncles, grandmothers and so forth) When we grow a society or culture, it makes a big difference in the organization, whether we use a male or a female point of view. Men want a hierarchical structure based on strength or force; women want a structure based on cohesiveness and harmony. Men have been dominant in society for the last 4500 years or so, but throughout most of ancient (2500BC) history, most societies were matrifocal. Matrifocal means that feminine thinking was central to every aspect of life. Feminine thinking was mixed with male thinking. It is not correct to say that these societies were woman-dominated, but rather that women contributed their full measure in partnership with men in the decision making process of those cultures.

The Paleolithic, Mesolithic, and Neolithic Ages lasted from approximately 2,000,000 to 2500 B.C. They were the late, middle and new stone ages. The archeological data clearly shows that man was not dominant over woman or vice versa in those times. The farther we go back in time, the more cooperative "society" was. Yes, life was simpler and gender roles were perhaps more clearly defined, but women were valued and involved in the process of running society of the day. Important decisions were made by both sexes in consultation with each other. One of the things most notable missing from Neolithic art are scenes of violence and warfare. Is this to say that warfare did not exist? No, but warfare was not glorified in their artistic expression. It has been said, that the true leaders of society are artists. This is because the artist dares to see a vision or raise the specter of possibility for tomorrow. Art really is our vision quest. And

WouldArt is on a new vision quest. The fact that violence and warfare are absent from Neolithic art speaks volumes about their gender mindset. Neolithic art was based upon goddess worship involving the mysteries surrounding birth, creation, abundance of food and death.

What we do see in the art and artifacts of the Copper Age and earlier periods are the peaceful concerns of life: raising crops, gathering food, having babies, coming to terms with death, and most of all goddess worship at the center of the community. It was the mother who was seen at the center of creation, not the father. From every corner of creation the female principle screams at us as the mechanism of propagation. Mother Earth, Mother Nature is the moving force on this planet. Life and death, the change of seasons, ebb and flow are more female than male principles.

These are the logical reasons early communities of human beings were matrifocal. Life was tenuous during the Stone and Bronze Ages, and communities needed all their resources and talents to keep themselves going. Early man knew that women were his true ally and a potent force. Men and women used each other and each was allowed to flourish. Women were responsible for the majority of the food that was gathered and eaten, and they created pottery, clothing and the earliest agricultural tools. Women, as always, were the vessels of new life. Whatever any of us thinks of women and their function; it is women who are responsible for the continuation of the species. Man plays a part in the propagation of the species, but it is a subordinate role. The heroine, of the birth process is a woman. The primary force of propulsion in Mother Nature is feminine.

In ancient times the Great Goddess was prayed to and worshipped. Now we have "God the Father". We don't see the male principle readily working in nature, but we ask for "Our Father's" blessing for all manner of things. An important point to note is that the Immortal Goddess of antiquity is missing from modern history. Who were the people who wrote history in the last 4500 years? Men. Is history all facts? No. History is a combination of fact, fiction, opinion and conjecture. He who is doing the conjuring is the one in control of the story, the one who writes his story - History. It is not surprising that the depiction of Neolithic history and Goddess worship was omitted from our historical understanding until recently. It simply does not fit the male model of the universe.

It is the creation of life that was the greatest mystery of early humankind. In the most ancient times neither men nor women knew the role sex played in the birth of a child, but people were in awe of the female capacity to create life. This is the central mystery at the base of all spiritual speculation. Because it addresses or begs the spiritual questions:

1. Who am I?
2. Where am I from?
3. Where am I going?

It seems very odd that we have gotten so far away from Goddess worship, because Mother God is much more approachable and understandable than Father God. We can see the mother principle at work in nature, the father input is not so visible and is subordinate.

The powerful phenomenon of childbirth overwhelms anyone, past or present. Our ancestors asked themselves, as we do today: "Who creates life? What is the creator of the world?" And the answer was then and now - the feminine principle. The magic of birth is awe-inspiring as is watching a plant come out of the earth. Seeing fruit form on a tree begs us to hear the song of our Mother Earth. Can you see and hear it?

Our ancestors revered women not only for producing babies, but also for guiding the community on the voyage of life. Power was inherent in women because the force of nature flowed through them. Women's "natural talents" for patience, nurture and love were viewed as the right qualities for a leader. Women used power judiciously in all areas of life because all of life was an extension of motherhood. Religion and government had strong female leadership because this was thought to be the safe and right place for power to originate. It wasn't man the hunter/warrior who was best suited to talk about life, but woman, the creator of babies.

In ancient times old women were charged with religious duties and were the keepers of the wisdom of right and wrong. It was the crone who gave us our first rules of conduct. It was the young mother who gave us love and the old mother who gave us wisdom. Men played their part, but mother love was the force that allowed us to emerge from the cave into a community. Love became the basis of mutual respect and friendship. Love gives us the ability to sit down in peace with another person. We learn how to love from our mothers. We don't learn love from a hunter/warrior.

The archetypal female, the prototype given to us from the force of Mother Nature, combined magic, mystery, prophecy, healing, fertility, birth and death. Women understood the seasonal changes and were responsible for producing a vital part of the sacred knowledge in Neolithic time. The metaphorical lifeblood of the community was associated with women's, menstrual and birth blood - literally. Women menstruated in synchronicity with the moon and each other. It was understood that pregnant women stopped menstruating because their sacred blood was being used to create the magic of a new life. In the old days when an aging mother stopped menstruating, it was assumed that the scared blood was being used for mysterious and magical purposes. Women had sacred blood, and old women were considered the wisest of all beings.

The menstrual and birth blood is an anchor, a bond, to the force of Mother Nature and human intelligence. The female mind contributes qualities that make us better, but we don't seem to realize or honor it today. The fact that menstruation is often times considered "the curse"; clearly shows how far off base we have come. Menstruation really is magic and we should appreciate this collective, synchronizing link to the force of nature. Maybe more women would think better of their menstruation, if they were respected for having it. If we had more awareness of the role of menstruation in human development, perhaps we would respect and appreciate ourselves better.

When force was not the dominant feature of culture, when reason and intuition were used to grasp the world instead of wrestling it into submission, women were a logical component in the leadership of society. This principle is still true today, but there are very few examples extant of matrifocal communities. The few that are left are usually very small, primitive and isolated. For example, in the Kalahari Bushmen and the Bambuti Pygmies of Africa, female thought is respected and both sexes cooperate with child raising. We should endeavor to understand the benefits of those cultures and their power-sharing in order to improve the quality of our own existence.

Very few people would deny that technology exists or disregard the benefits of science and industry. Our challenge is not to be "primitive" and get in touch with Mother Nature by running around in the woods in our bare feet. Our job is to understand the functionality and beauty in the human design and to get all the parts working together in a coherent fashion.

Human potential has divine origins and expectations. (Assumption 347.514) However, nothing is earned without effort. If we cannot keep this world the paradise it already is, we don't deserve to be here. It is our job to understand our destiny and devise a practical path towards it. We deserve nothing else but what we produce for ourselves.

Death – Misogyny - Matrifocal Society

A universal sentiment, sometimes strong and sometimes weak, exists among men to resent women. There is a natural antagonism between men and women. Men are hard and forceful; women are soft and subtle. In the recesses of collective consciousness of man is a true hatred of women. This is not a rational thought, but a gut feeling that men have. This hatred is a matter of degree, circumstance and does vary with time and circumstance. Of course this hatred is mixed with love and admiration and a whole host of other thoughts and feelings. The same is true for women hating and loving men. Men do not understand women, and women do not understand men.

One of the biggest reasons for misogyny, the hatred and persecution of women, is men's fear and denial of death. In nature, we cannot have life without death. All of organic life is parasitic: everything lives off something else. We live on a planet that is itself organic and "things" survive off the plants and animals that surround us. We usually think of parasites as nasty little creatures like fleas or leaches, but we humans are no different in sucking the life's blood out of our host. There really is nothing wrong with being parasitic as long as we don't kill or cripple the host. What Mother Nature teaches us is that death is a part of life; Mother Nature uses death in order to nurture and enhance life.

Women are responsible for carrying human life, and because of the close relationship between life and death, women are also associated with death. In an archetypal part of the human mind women are responsible for death. The woman is associated with the womb of birth; the womb of the unconscious; the womb of death. The womb of our creation mysteries is associated with women and begs the question of our uncreation - Death.

In many different cultures and at many times in history, women, and reproductive parts have been associated with death. Woman is responsible for the "little castration or little death" that occurs after a male climax. It is the women who are sucking (robbing) the life forces from the man. It is the insatiable vagina that takes the strong man and reduces him to nothing, and in the process sapping the vital spirit that makes man strong. Isn't this the reason women live longer? Isn't this one of the arguments for celibacy? Celibacy gives one the energy for more spiritual pursuits. The toothless mouth of female genitals is the gateway to both heaven and hell for a man.

Another reason for misogyny is the burden a woman creates. The very presence of a woman is a challenge to a man. "Can you help me, hold me, and support me and my children"? Much of men's hatred, persecution and resentment of women; comes from the burdens they associate with the female. Men fear the burden women present. Men are biologically drawn to women, but have a psychological fear of them. The vagina forces most men to behave irrationally the majority of their lives. Most all men want love and sexual companionship, but have a hard time with the consuming psychological embrace that most women demand. Men love women and sex, but there is a price to pay.

Negative emotions are also generated from men's envy of women's power in life, birth and creation. Freud's theory of penis envy is really just an envy of men's power in the modern world, not of men's anatomy. However, there is at least some level of male resentment towards women's real power in creating and sustaining life. For me, the most powerful experiences of my life were watching the births of my two daughters, and I can only imagine the exaltation of actually giving birth. Although I knew it was no easy task, I was envious of the experience. I was envious of not being able to breastfeed a child. I don't think anyone can establish a closer bond than the mother and child through

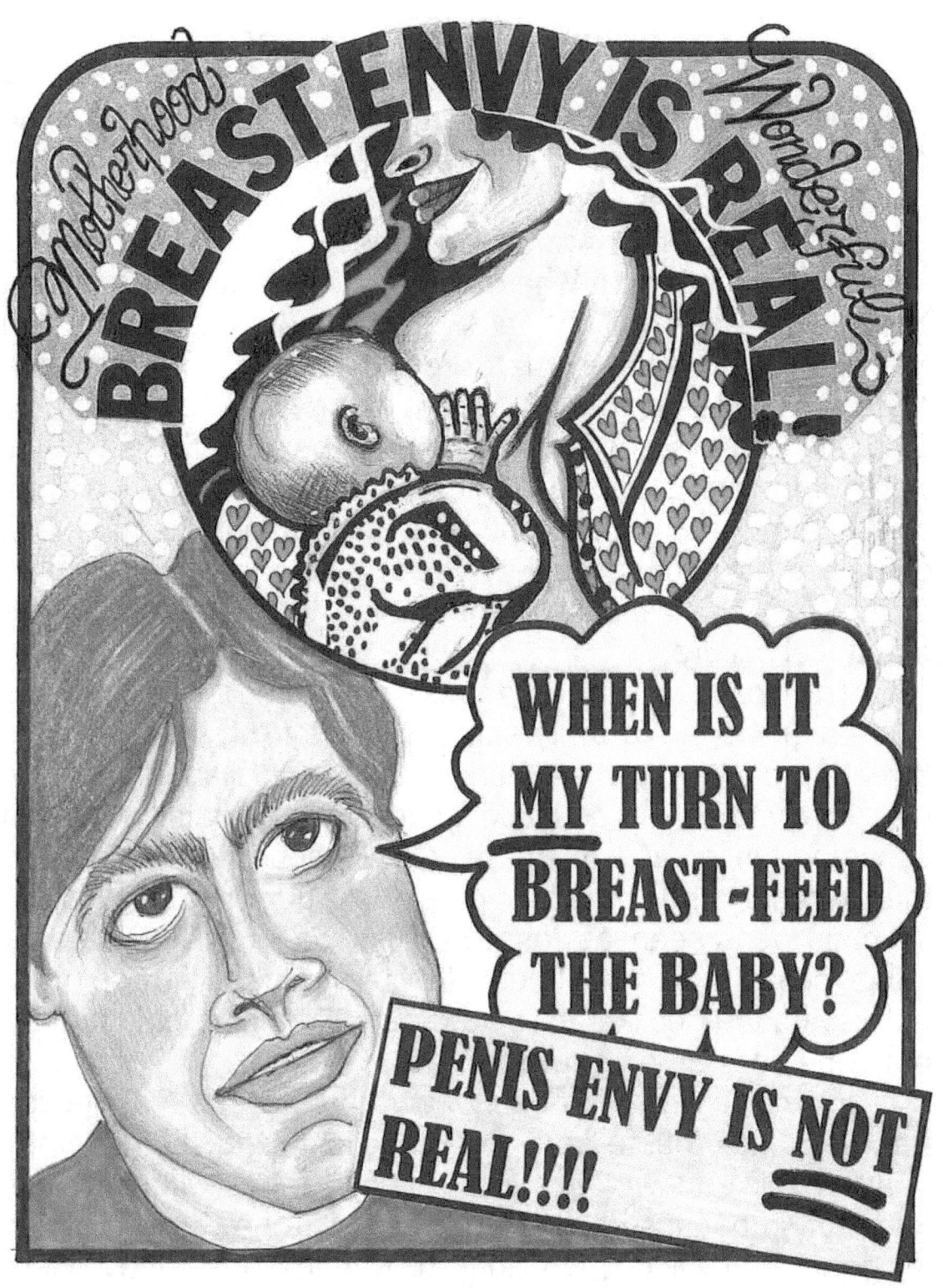

breastfeeding. Breast envy is very real but not widely appreciated.

Matrifocal Societies Decline

Death and birth are part of the dynamic in the psychological pathology between the sexes. Why were matrifocal societies almost destroyed and forgotten? It is difficult to know how things were because the evidence is gone and the male dominate view of today filters everything we see. The prevailing paradigm is that male-dominated culture is the natural human order. The available evidence and common sense do not support this point of view. The archeological evidence, now, clearly shows the first societies were matriarchal. The study of insect and animal communities does not reveal male domination. We must ask ourselves how human society became patriarchal. Four main factors (assumption 352.3) contributed to the demise of the matrifocal culture.

The first factor in the demise of the maternal clan was when men began to understand that they had something to do with producing babies. Early man's understanding that he was involved in reproduction gave him a greater sense of self-importance, and in his mind it lessened or diminished the miracle and mystery of birth surrounding women. Women were seen as less powerful and under the same influences of nature as men; they no longer were seen as not having the godlike ability to create life alone, but just part of the process of reproduction.

Women were probably aware of the connection between intercourse and reproduction long before they shared this knowledge with men. They withheld this information because it created a sense of power for women in general. Giving men the knowledge that they were involved in reproduction would diminish the female as sole creator. All religion up until that time venerated the female principle of creation, and there was no recognition of any paternal participation. There was probably an element of male resentment because men felt that the withheld knowledge was a means of imprisonment and discrimination, which it was. The same ploy is used in reverse today when women and minorities are told that they "can't do something because only a man can do that job," or "only a white man is capable of that kind of work."

The second reason for the decline of the matrifocal society has to do with technology. As the Bronze Age gave way to the Age of Iron, new and better weapons, with more effective methods of deployment and delivery, were developed. Better weaponry allowed warfare to be elevated to the status of science. It was the development of metallurgy as a male dominated craft that literally and figuratively catapulted men into positions of leadership. The concept of "to the victory belong the spoils" came of age. An appetite for "The Spoils" helped diminish the Mother/Goddess culture. The time of the professional warrior, shifting from a tribal defensiveness, had come to pass.

Concurrent with the advancement of technology was the improvement in transportation. People were getting around better with the domestication of the horse and camel. With iron technology better tools were invented which allowed the building of bigger and better ships and other vehicles of transportation and war. If one can ride to a distant location and not be tired, fighting becomes more feasible. If you have to walk twenty-five miles in a day, at the end of the day you don't feel much like fighting.

The Iron Age warrior had an inflated sense of himself from the dramatically increased power of his weaponry and his knowledge of paternity. This warrior was surrounded by people who did not have his knowledge or his weapons. In other words, they were easy prey. This warrior could not, or did not, resist going out and taking what he wanted. The world was viewed as a place to be conquered and dominated instead of lived in peacefully. This was perhaps the greatest and most tragic revolution of all time. Man's neighbor began to be seen as easy prey.

It is the combination of these factors that ushered in the decline of matrifocal society that produced the third reason for change to patriarchy, religious doctrine. When early man realized that he had something to do with making babies, he also realized that a father figure was missing from his religious beliefs. Some adjustment in theology to include a father figure was inevitable at this point.

With Iron Age technology man created superior weapons of destruction, allowing for a phenomenon that had not previously existed on a large scale: war. Warfare needed some kind of moral justification, which clearly did not exist in Goddess theology. Therefore, a further adjustment to the theology of the time required a father figure who also was a god of war. A vengeful God gave good reason to send men out to conquer and kill. This God had to be cleverly disguised as noble and holy; he was not motivated by the "spoils of victory". This new male God exhorted his followers to stomp out previous pagan thinking. Any means is justified in a holy war. Early man must have had a difficult time justifying himself in a society with a long history of peaceful co-existence with neighbors. On the other hand, the man with the sword had the power to impose his will on a large number of people. Might makes right has always been a difficult thesis to oppose.

Religion provides the foundation from which cultural and social customs are regulated. It is religion that sets the boundaries of moral and ethical thinking, and this thinking establishes the framework upon which secular laws are written. Theology is really a social, economic and political strategy. It has always been true that philosophy was the first science. Religion is the first philosophy. It has been said that we are the only animal species that weave stories that guide our behavior. By changing the structure of theology from matriarchal to patriarchal, man was able to justify and legitimize his behavior regarding warfare. Iron Age man wrote a script that allowed him to destroy all pagan religions and cultures. He had to obey his God and conquer the world over and over again. Religious warfare of today still demands we wipe out infidels and heretics.

The fourth and final reason that matrifocal societies became nearly extinct is that they had no mechanism of defense. The very nature of Goddess culture was peaceful. Goddess culture had no defense because they had no desire for offense. Matrifocal societies are programmed with the values of nurturing, caring and cohesiveness. Warfare is inconsistent with these values. A fatal flaw in the design of Goddess culture is that it could not protect or defend itself. This dilemma lives with us today and will haunt humankind for all eternity or our extinction whichever comes first.

The question we have to ask ourselves is do we want peaceful coexistence on this planet? Many people who will answer this question throughout the world today will say – NO. It is a harsh reality that violent, self destructive people, groups, governments and societies are with us now. If peace is to prevail; we will have to overcome each opposing force on a case by case basis. The road to "peace on Earth" is not easy or certain.

Chapter three

Male Characteristics

Male Characteristics

The biggest psychological difference between the sexes is the way they think. Men and women live in separate psychological and sociological environments and their brains are different - physiologically. As a result men solve problems differently from women. In this chapter we will examine some of the characteristics that demonstrate these differences from a male perspective. By understanding the dynamics of male thinking better, we can more effectively deal with it. A number of hypotheses presented herein are based upon personal observations and experiences that will hopefully ring true for you.

A lot of men's thinking is connected to their bodies as it relates to physical strength. Men really live in their bodies on a primal level. A man takes pride in his physicality and derives a sense of prowess from his body. Part of the archetype of the male psyche is the image of man as the warrior/hunter. It does not matter if a man is short or tall, weak or strong in stature. Men see themselves as dominating figures because they associate themselves with the warrior/hunter masculine archetype that has been defined by biology and cultural tradition. The archetype is a primal sense or recollection from the ancient past as well as a current conception. Men are taught and continue to see themselves as warrior/hunters regardless of their station in life. It does not matter if a man is a banker, baker or candlestick maker; men are all warrior/hunters in their own eyes.

Man has the body type that is cultured to be the defender. Man is also cultured to be the provider. The warrior/hunter masculine archetype is also defined, in part, by comparison with women and, in part, by comparison with other men. Woman, generally, do not have parity in physical strength with men. Therefore, women are not usually in competition on a physical basis with men. Males usually

obtain a great deal of their self-esteem and self-worth through their bodily strength in relation to women as well as to other men. The reason for comparison with women is that it is almost always favorable for men. Of course men compare themselves to other men too, but those comparisons can be humbling. So, a comparison with women is a sure fired winner for a man. A man showing women and children their muscles is something that can generally be counted on for esteem building results. Most men demonstrate their physical strength, overtly or subtlety, to the woman and children around them regularly and to other men when it is advantageous.

Men have another curious predilection that is associated with physical strength. For many men, there is a causal relationship between physical strength and intellectual self-perception. Men make an associative leap from the strength of their physical body to the strength of their mental body. Men generally have the notion that because they are larger and stronger than females or other men, they are intellectually stronger as well. Man sees himself as mentally strong as a function of his physical self-perception.

Being physically strong is what the primal man is supposed to be. From this model he leaps to the assumption of intellectual, psychological and spiritual superiority. This is aptly summed up in the saying "might makes right." This does not mean to say that men feel superior to women solely on the basis that they are stronger, but this fact contributes a great deal to the assumption. Most importantly, physical strength allows men to impose their will and ideas on women and other men. We live in a might makes right world.

Man's superior fighting/warrior skill is the mechanism by which he can assert his "rights" over weaker women and men. Superior force is confused with superior rights. "Rights" in this context is a euphemism for desire or will. A man can use aggression to force his authority and "righteousness."

When a conflict arises, a man can employ superior force instead of superior logic to get his way. For many men superior force is superior logic. Using a loud voice is often enough to put an idea across. Ideas with physical force behind them can easily supplant better ideas. No one has to look far for examples of might-makes-right behavior. War is the grossest manifestation of might makes right. The might makes right principle translates to each and every one of us on a personal level. We all use physical, verbal, psychological, social, political, intellectual, or economic force to enforce a point of view. We use these forces singularly or in combinations. Physical prowess is the trump card of force. Men use force more often than women because it works. Men use their physical force trump card to get what they want, because they can.

Transfer of Training

There is a concept in psychology describing this behavior called "transfer of training". This is the process of taking behaviors or principles learned in one aspect of life and employing them in another. Transfer of training is usually associated with behavior that is true, such as mathematical ability used to enhance musical talent. However, in the instance of men's physical and mental strength, we are dealing with a perceived truth. Some men use force to convince themselves and women they have superior brains. Force is defined in the context of a superior position in the physical, economic and or political circumstance. Force does not make men smarter. Force is confused with intelligence because it can be imposed. Force is often successful in intellectual disputes because it is able to "enforce" itself. Therefore, men have been able to transfer their physical strength skill into the arena of mental strength.

Many play into and support this kind of reasoning. For example, a husband yells at his wife, or a father threatens

his children to convince them to do what he thinks is right. If the yelling fails the male may resort to more physical force. There is no question that yelling, threatening and physical force do work, but sometimes they backfire. Men often find themselves apologizing for something they forced on others. At other times they find themselves suffering consequences when they cannot correct or take back their actions. The reverse is also true. Men will occasionally submit to the aggressive forcefulness of a wife or children. For the most part, however, since a man's physical stature is greater than theirs, the man is not as easily intimidated by their methods of force. They do not usually have the trump card of using physical force to enforce a point.

Everyone participates in the deception of enforced ideas or policies at one time or another. We force children to do things, which may or may not be good for them. We tell them "It's for your own good," but men use physical intimidation, significantly more than women, to impose their point of view. Might makes right.

War has always been the medium most successfully associated with imposing control on others by using physical force. If someone confronts you and says, "I will blow your head off if you do not agree with me," chances are good you will think about complying. If enough force is applied, anyone can be made to agree with a demand. The science of war has taught us how to get our way. War and its associated activities are powerful mechanisms that help to keep women in positions of subservience and out of the power structure.

Men fear being dominated by other men and women, so they use aggressive, forceful behavior in order to forestall others from dominating them. From childhood men learn the tactics of how to be physically aggressive in order to obtain power. The male mindset is infused with the expediency and mechanics of might makes right. Using force is seen as tactic or tool and a right of passage.

The ritual of aggressive, forceful individual behavior can grow and mutate into group domination and eventually warfare. Warfare is considered to be a rite of passage for males in almost all cultures; it is purported to build character and give one a sense of manhood. Warfare is thought to refine a man's mettle by testing his ability to endure pain and suffering and inflict the same or worse on others. It is often asserted that war is hell, but it builds character and leadership in a man. However, in reality, war makes a person crueler and more violent than he normally would be. Are these the characteristics we want in our leaders? What are a military man's qualifications for leadership? Military leaders have good organization skills and the ability to look ahead and plan strategies for victory. However, the military man has also demonstrated the ability and willingness to kill people and direct others to kill; to win at any cost. Military leaders throughout history have either taken political power by force or have had it handed to them. Is a military mind the ideal candidate for political leadership? On principle I would say no. Perhaps such leaders should be disqualified from civic leadership. A man or woman with blood on their hands is dangerous. Professional killers with an ethic of "win at any price"; does not seem like the ideal civic leader. At the very least we should carefully consider, on a case by case basis, each military person for political office.

Many men have a preoccupation with direct or vicarious violence. Men are programmed from the time that they are children to be warriors and hunters – killers. Human beings are animals. We kill other animals including other human beings to survive. It is a fact of nature. The problem is that the stakes are getting very high. We are at a crossroads in our evolution. We have evolved to the point where we can destroy the world. We have to change the human predilection for violence before we destroy ourselves.

We are not solely beasts anymore. Humans have made steps forward in civilization and civility. Some claim that

sports have helped us a great deal in the transition from a beast to a social being. The theory is that playing or watching violent sports has abated the urge to actually kill others in real time. Men vicariously experience the ritual of war by watching or participating in sports. Most violent sports are played almost exclusively by men. Football, hockey, hunting, rugby, boxing, and video games are all either directly or indirectly violent. In our society today, most men are deprived of the real experience of war. However, men still crave the "combat encounter" and get satiated from the vicarious experiences of war and violence in sports and entertainment.

"Might makes right" thinking is part of our heritage. On some level we probably still need violent sports and entertainment in order to wean, us men, from our killer instincts. As a species we seem addicted to violence. We have made strides in human history towards an understanding that violence is not inevitable, but optional. How violent we are always depends on the circumstance we find ourselves in. The terrorist attack on America at the World Trade Towers in New York City on September 11, 2001 gave us pause on the one hand and on the other hand brought out mighty thoughts of revenge. Right after 9/11 normally nonviolent people talked about "getting even." The Patriot Act and the invasion of Afghanistan sailed through both houses of congress.

Print, video and internet news sources elevate stories of violence to positions of prominence. The stories are all pretty much alike; just the faces, places and names change but the brutality is the same. They play a significant part in the way we think about the world. We are programmed by what we see in the news. "A man is not what he thinks he is, but what he thinks, he is."[1] We are a violent society in large

---

[1] quote by Max R. Hickerson

part because we are fed violence constantly by our information sources.

The news media play to our weaknesses and feed violence to us as if we were addicts. In a sense we may well be characterized as addicts. The more sensational, violent and bizarre the news stories, the more we crave them. We have been programmed to accept them as news, but in reality they are dramas designed to catch and focus our attention to sell advertising.

Violence is a fact of life, but it is reported way out of proportion to its occurrence in society. How many murders have you, personally, seen in real life? Have you personally known someone who was murdered? The average person does not come in contact with violence and brutality on a daily basis in real time. Most people see murder, rape and pillaging, everyday, because we read newspapers, watch television or go to the movies. The News media hunts for sensational stories of bizarreness and violence and then feeds us their catch.

GANGS

Gangs have been around in society for many generations, but their current extent is unprecedented. Gangs are everywhere in the world, in small towns as well as large, high income and low-income neighborhoods. Their prevalence is a symptom of imbalances in society. Gangs and their violent behavior tell us much about the dysfunctional aspects of our culture. First and foremost, gangs are surrogate families. They provide the bonding that should take place in the family. However, the traditional family in which a father and mother provide and take care of the family has all but ceased to exist. Single and working parents have a difficult time providing the time and direction necessary for raising their children. Without responsible adult guidance, recognition and acknowledgment, the young turn to gangs for guidance and attention.

Gangs fill the void left by absent parents. They form a peer group that may even forge a blood bond with a young person and profess loyalty to the death. They can also provide the mechanism for making a lot of money and gaining status and prestige in the greater community. They provide guidance, recognition, excitement and usually large financial incentives through involvement with drugs, and they are accessible and easy to join. Those who join gangs don't have to be smart or work hard to reap big rewards – just willing.

Gangs provide a channel for violence and anger. Many young people feel isolated, frustrated and full of anger. Anger asks for an outlet. Previous generations also had anger, but they had the ability to release their frustration in warfare or hunting. Because warfare has become suicidal on the global stage, it is becoming rare or obsolete in American society, and hunting is not an option for most urban kids. Meat comes from the supermarket.

Young males still have a desire to test their mettle in some form; the archetypical man still exists. Gangs create their own war scenarios and fill a need for a life-and-death challenge. Long periods of peace and no hunting are a relatively new development, and many people, particularly young American males, have a difficult time adjusting to it. Gang violence is a way of creating the warfare/hunt experience that society is not providing.

Like the canary bird in the mining operation, gangs are acting as warning signals of the breakdown of our social fabric. Gang proliferation tells us that society is not working for a large and vital part of our culture; they are an adolescent solution to problems that originate in the adult world. We need to understand the void that gangs are attempting to fill and bridge the gap in meaningful ways.

An important aspect of addressing the problem of violence in society is the acknowledgment of our appetite for it. Men, much more than women, have a desire for violence. Aggression and violence seem to be built into the male machinery of thinking. Violence, either direct or indirect seems to have a correlation with intimacy for many men. Men get close to other men by playing or watching football together, or by being in an army platoon, gang, or hunting club. In essence a team, platoon, gang or club is a displaced family, a place for affiliation, association, and intimacy. If we understood the dynamic of intimacy better, perhaps we could take care of the underlying needs that compel some to join such groups to avoid rejection and alienation. By joining groups we prevent one of our greatest fears, isolation, and take care of one of our greatest needs, intimacy.

As a society we need to mitigate and transform the need for violence. We need to channel our violent tendencies into activities that do not promote our own and society's self-destruction. Conquering and fighting is an extension of supporting/defending the family. Supporting a family requires the destruction of animals, plants, trees, the environment, etc. A short step from fighting for survival is arrogant, aggressive and hostile behavior that goes beyond supporting the family. The family becomes attached to a tribe, and then to a community, a state, and a nation, and the degree of allowable destructive behavior becomes greater as the group becomes larger.

Hostile, destructive behavior becomes sanctioned as a function of family/planetary support. Man is allowed, even encouraged, to become destructive as long as it has some association with the continuation of the group. Governments sanction violence and destruction. This is the reason the oceans fish and the rain forests are being depleted.

Man's need to dominate and subordinate others is related to how men see themselves physically--that is, in competition with existing forces both real and imagined. Men generally orient themselves in business, government, sex, language, etc. so that they can dominate and subordinate others. This is a mechanism that men use to gain self-esteem. However, there is a down side to the extremes of male competitiveness; the precarious state of the world is the result of male domination rather than cooperation and mutual benefit. To understand this concept better look at male sexual behavior.

Male sexuality

In traditional male/female sexual interaction, it is the man who usually initiates the activity. The male mounts his female in a characteristic dominating fashion. He penetrates and invades the woman with the feeling that he is conquering this individual. He is now in control, dominating and subduing her and taking his pleasure in the process. This generic man consummates his pleasure in a mist of thinking that he has performed his job well, oblivious to the fact that he has left his woman without satisfaction. Because man merely dominates and uses his sexual partner, he fails to appreciate the benefits of cooperation. Is not the same thesis true with men in business, government and other areas of male/female interaction? Men do not generally understand the female sexual dynamic and therefore do not gain an appreciation for mutual satisfaction and enhancement.

It is male arrogance that has kept him ignorant of female sexuality. Straight men fail to satisfy women sexually because they confuse the goal (climax) with the process. Many women do not live for the climax in sex; they crave the entire embrace in which the climax is part of the finale. For a woman, the finale in the drama of sex has little meaning if it is not coherently associated with a psychological as well as a physical sequence of events. The sequence of events for a woman is one in which the drama has a beginning, a middle and an end and is set within the context of an entire life story.

Some men isolate love and affection from the sex experience entirely. Some focus their male energy on the physical towards a climax. Some men become so self-centered that they are simply pulsating penises who receive self pleasure not associated with a partner, life story or social dynamic. Love is not usually present at all, but ignored or suppressed. Climax-oriented men think of themselves as pleasure conduits who do not think of their partner.

A man has two sensuous drivers located at opposite ends of his torso. The head on his neck is capable of thinking and the other driver is sexual. Each part influences the other. At any given time either driver is capable of taking control and running the show. Part of the mystery of life is that we never know which head will take charge at any given moment.

As men become more aware of the needs of others, their behavior will change based upon increased sensitivities. Women's awareness and sensitivity allow them the superior perspective that sex can be part of a loving life song in which the self is an instrumental part.

Men who fail to appreciate the feminine capacity in both sex and decision-making do not get the best results in either arena. In sex some men do not ask their partners what they want or how to improve the experience. In the world of public policy, business, and religion, women are excluded in the

same regard as they are in the sex experience. The psychological dynamics that keep men from desiring better sex and better problem solving are pride and fear, opposite sides of the same coin. Some men are willing to settle for a feeling of superiority as opposed to the reality of excellence. If a man thinks he has performed well, it is good enough. Men do not want to hear any criticism about their sexual performance. It diminishes the experience. At issue is man's pride in thinking he has adequately performed sexually, and his fear of seeing himself as deficient. Men are caught in a dilemma of feeling insecure about their sexual performance and not disturbing the status quo. They also enjoy the activity the way it is. Thus, many men lack the courage to resolve this dilemma, not realizing that increased sexual sensitivity to their mates would also increase their own pleasure and fulfillment.

In the intellectual realm some men will deny the veracity and cogency of women's thinking in order to bolster the strength of their own thoughts. Their insecurity denies the ability to appreciate the antithesis of any position. Sometimes males are threatened by female thinking. Women's thinking tends not to involve force, aggression or coercion. Force is almost synonymous with male characteristics. Consequently, men are not comfortable with female solutions because it means denying the characteristics that identify maleness. Not hearing women in matters of public policy shows a lack of confidence and courage on man's part. It has always been easy to say that women are not good mathematicians and engineers, or that they cannot wage war properly. The truth of the matter is that women have not had as much opportunity, so we do not know what performance characteristics they possess or whether their ideas will improve our lives or not. The performance characteristics are especially true in matters of public policy. We are, however, certain that male performance characteristics in public policy are terrible.

By denying women an equal share in decision-making, men become blind to their own weaknesses. Not being able to acknowledge weakness is one of the greatest liabilities anyone can have. When men censor women's decisions they prohibit self-understanding. Many men do not want to divulge personal weakness, share or give power away or lose the upper hand even if it means supporting a policy that is not good.

In general, men are reluctant to discuss their weaknesses, particularly about sex, because they think it will reduce their power. Sex is a source of power for men and can be a cause for insecurity. Some men think that discussing personal problems and feelings will reveal and weaken them. In fact, not talking is a great weakness in itself. Not being willing to analyze oneself or to conceal information is not a position of strength.

The male idealized image is to be strong, capable and self-reliant. Many times this male image is more form that fact. A man has to project and prove himself if he wants a wife (sex), stature among other males, possessions, and the power to rule others. Insecurity about achieving the above-mentioned goals is one of man's strongest driving forces, and insecurity demands attention. If we are insecure about not having something, we think about it. If we are not able to satiate a desire or need, we compensate for it. Some of our compensation for insecurity takes the form of concealment. If we cannot deal with our own deficiencies directly, we hide from them. Violence is a way to express frustration and to conceal problems with sex, money, whatever - from others and also from ourselves.

Men have a greater proclivity to use violence, force and other methods of concealment than women. The reason is because men have a greater ego investment in being right or "in control". Man controls more of the physical world and is predominately responsible for what is - both right and wrong – in our governing of the world. This idea is true on an

CLOSET of CONCEALMENT

individual and global scale. Men are prone to conceal their personal problems from themselves and others, and male world leaders hide planetary problems from the public and themselves.

A Frontline[2] documentary about the Rocky Flats nuclear weapons factory in Colorado perfectly illustrates this point. Rocky Flats was and is an ecological disaster of titanic proportions. Plutonium contamination is everywhere, enough to kill the entire world many times over. When workers stepped forward to complain, they were censored and sabotaged. A grand jury was convened to investigate the situation, and they recommended criminal indictments against Rockwell International. The Rockwell employees who simply talked to the grand jury put their livelihood and lives in jeopardy. The grand jury found evidence of pollution activity on a scale that can only be called "crimes against humanity". Before a trial could begin, Rockwell obtained a plea bargain with the Department of Justice and Energy. The grand jury was told to pack up, go home and not talk about the case at the risk of prosecution. Rockwell got a slap on the wrist (an $18,000,000 fine and no criminal charges or culpability), and the Departments of Justice and Energy have made statements that everything is now all right. The fact of the matter is that Rocky Flats is an ecological time bomb.

Neither government nor business wanted to deal with the environmental crisis, so they put a shroud over the whole thing. The Rocky Flats issue is not much different from the way a lot of men deal with personal problems. It is considered foolish to divulge information about one's "shortcomings". Men hide information from others and themselves all the time. We may have homosexuals in the military, but our official policy is not to talk about it. Obviously this policy is inconsistent, but it is typical of a male propensity to hide issues that threaten "manhood".

---

[2] broadcast on P.B.S. television (KRCB) 10/28/93

How do we account for the Savings & Loan crisis, the biggest bank robbery in the history of the world, for which nobody is held accountable? What about the infrastructure in many American cities in which bridges crumble because they are not painted? At the Rio Summit, President Bush, Sr. had the opportunity to create some real consensus and policy for world environmental issues. He chose the opposite and nothing happened. Are these kinds of problems too difficult to handle? Obviously not; the government at all levels is hiding important issues. I think the problem for men is they are out of synch with the masculine archetype. The real archetypal man is physically and mentally strong and faces his problems without flinching. Modern man is playing hide and seek with numerous important issues. When issues seem overwhelming or conflicting, the facts are ignored to maintain a facade of strength. Image is substituted for reality.

Homosexuality

Homosexuality reveals human nature on many levels. If we look analytically at homosexual behavior we can learn a great deal about some strengths and weakness in our species. I am a straight sexual person with experiences and perspective. My intention and hope is to shake some understanding loose from the tree of knowledge. Gay bashing is a type of gender discrimination. Homosexual people are just people, some good, some bad but most a mixture of both characteristics. I endorse love anywhere you can find it, and generally speaking, any love is better than no love – be it homosexual or heterosexual.

In my life I have noticed that a high percentage of straight men are generally threatened by homosexual men. The gay issue is volatile for straight men on a number of points. Among many straight men, the hatred of gays borders on paranoia. Gay bashing is very common. I have seen a lot of it over the years. Also, homosexual prejudice is written into the English language – cocksucker – faggot – queer, and is used to describe and demean. The gay man is perceived as flawed, but also as if he had a contagious disease. The disease is not physical but is portrayed as a mental abnormality. Some gay men have an expressed feminine side to their personalities that straight men resent. The big question comes to mind – why are gays so resented? One obvious answer is that the straight man has a fear of becoming gay. There is a feminine side to men, all men, which many men deny and fear. Do men enjoy/crave having their penis sucked? Does rain come from the sky? Most all men crave oral sex and the provider can be male or female. It is very easy to have homosexual experiences.

For the gay man, the female body is not required for sex. For many a straight guy, the female mind is not necessary for sex, just the body. In straight thinking the gay man represents their ultimate sexual failure with women. The fact that the gay man does not see women as sexual objects is antithetical to straight male thinking. As a result, many men develop anger towards gays because they do not confirm straight sex thinking. To be sexually adequate with women a man must literally "rise" to the occasion. Most men fear sexual failure. With straight men, sexual failure with women is horrible. Sexual failure makes anyone feel inadequate. Inadequacy is what straight men associate with gays. Gay men are portrayed as failing sexually with women. Gay men choose not to engage women sexually. This is a gay male preference or choice. Therefore the gay man is resented and demeaned for being a sexual failure and for making a wrong choice.

In straight thinking, gay men are not whole people; they are sexually and psychologically deficient. Also, women are not whole people; they are sexual objects. Hating gays and demeaning women is not unreasonable to many a straight male mind. This prejudice is superficial, but it is very pervasive. If we really look at what this prejudice holds, the issue is not about another's choices and predilections; it's about our own feelings of inadequacy. The gay hater really has doubts about his or her own psychological and sexual adequacy.

The gay man is viewed as psychologically inferior and is placed in a parallel or lesser category with women. The condemnation of "queers" is a way of improving one's stature in one's own eyes and with others of a like mind. Persecuting others is an ancient human art form practiced by all but done insidiously well by the straight male power structure. Diminishing others has many functions, not the least of which is transferring blame and guilt. Gays become scapegoats and a means of clouding the issue of male/female sexual dysfunction. Calling someone "faggot" or "cocksucker" can usually keep our attention away from the real issues. Gay bashing is an accepted way of channeling aggression and relieving stress.

Homosexual men are a masculine bridge to feminine thinking and characteristics. The gay man is aware he is not part of the "established order", in much the same way that women are excluded. Even if they belong to the "inner circle", a gay man or women knows they are usually only tolerated and token. The gay man plays a game of concealment or confrontation with the straight male world, because it is hostile to him. Gay men have learned the pain of persecution over centuries of being left out of the "established" loop. Being persecuted or ignored is a shared experience that can produce an understanding and empathy between women and gay men. A further empathy is developed because gay men do not threaten women sexually, which lessens the sexual tension between them. The opposite is also true; tension between gay and straight men is increased because the potential for sex exists.

The gay man has developed a wariness but also a sensitivity to others because they are part of a persecuted class, just like women. Homosexual phobia is revealing of insecurity in the straight male mindset. Women are not as condemning of homosexual behavior because women have empathy. Women have been persecuted and have a distinct distaste for it. Women tend to be tolerant because it is necessary to be an accepting mother. Motherhood is an education in acceptance that has an enormous strength that helps hold humanity together. Women get along with gay men in large part because they are not sexual objects to them.

Homosexual people are insecure as individuals in a number of ways. Gay persecution is real in all parts of the world. Homosexual people are a minority – anywhere from 4 to 10 percent, depending on the study. Gay males are insecure because of the high rate of HIV in their community. The choice of sexual behavior means a smaller group of potential partners to choose from. And risk of deadly infection.

Homosexuality is chosen, rather than genetically determined. If we reduce sex to its mechanical operations perhaps we can understand the "choice thesis" better. From a mechanical point of view there is no difference between a wet orifice – male or female. It seems there is a preference for a personality associated with a gender. What is the difference between a male and female mouth or anis? Both are just orifices that are connected to a gender. What there is, is a psychological propensity – a choice or preference, to access an orifice associated with a gender. The homosexual decision seems a function of choice rather than genetics.

Another observation for many gay people is a troubled relationship with the opposite sex parent. Distorted relationships between a mother and son or between a father and daughter are common for homosexuals. The primary role model for the opposite sex is our parents. Some people feel compelled to same sex relationships because of oppressive parents modeling. If it is difficult to exist around an opposite sex parent, the role model for that opposite gender becomes warped and it influences a causal relationship. How we perceive a man or woman is modeled for us first by our parents. Parents become the standard by which we gauge others.

Homosexuals seem more self-absorbed with self-centered behavior than people in general. Perhaps gay people are more self-centered because they do not generally have children and learn the lessons of self-sacrifice. Not having children makes it much more difficult to fully understand the deepest aspects of sharing and giving. After having a child, most people would not hesitate to give their life to save their child. Giving your life is the ultimate test of love. Children and self sacrifice go hand in hand. There is a natural connection between children, love and sacrifice that is difficult to obtain other than by parenting experience.

Additionally gay people are more self-centered because they are a persecuted people in society. Self-love is a form of self-protection. It is like a shield that protects one from oncoming forces. It makes a great deal of sense that if "the world does not love me, my type, I will love my self and others who are like me". We all need love, and if the only love you can find is gay love – I say God bless it!

A number of gay people have moved from the heterosexual camp into the homosexual world. People who were once straight but are now gay. I get a strong sense, particularly from the women I have encountered, that it is a reaction to an emotional deprivation. There was a failure to get emotional needs meet. I hear straight people talking all the time that their wants are not being met by their mates. Is it true that men understand men better than women understand men? Yes! This point is overwhelmingly true about male's sexual needs. Women do not understand male sexual needs. And, men do not generally appreciate women's sexual needs. Women know women better than they know men, and vice versa. We all crave to be heard, to be reached by our significant other. If being in a heterosexual relationship feels like an emotional vacuum, maybe it is better to switch. If I had failure after failure, emotionally, in a straight relationship; I would feel marooned.

The touching of sexual behavior is just a front for emotional bonding. Human beings need to be touched in order to be happy. If we cannot psychologically bond to anyone from the opposite sex, then we seek love where we can. We need someone to physically stroke us and say – "I know you, you are special, I love you the way you are". Sex is not always the point; it is love that we crave. If I cannot get love from the opposite sex but can from my same gender; the choice becomes compelling.

In some ways gay people are more sensitive and loving than people in the straight world. Perhaps this is attributable to the pain of discrimination they are subjected to? They learn empathy and compassion the hard way, just like women – through persecution. Sensitivity for other people's pain is associated with their own pain/rejection. Persecution breeds empathy. The gay mindset is complex psychologically, but usually very tender and compassionate.

The dilemma for gays is to grow past self-love to a more mature love beyond the self. Most gays do not produce children. There really is a function to children. When they are our responsibility they push us past our own desires and boundaries. This is immensely profound and important. Striving for another is the basis of family, community and civilization. To give beyond one's self and to sacrifice for another is a hallmark of psychological maturity. Not everyone who has children is psychologically mature, but children pave the way towards maturity. Gays who do produce or have children are more apt to be psychologically mature. All of us are in a process of maturation. We are all looking at what works well and what does not, as part of the learning/maturing process. As a species we have a long way

to go. As individuals we are on a continuum towards greater and greater maturation. There is hope for us all.

Many gay people have a strong artistic affiliation. Taking pride in ones appearance is an artistic endeavor. A person who loves and embellishes himself has developed a skill in adornment and decoration. The gay mindset can teach us a lot about human nature as it relates to gender discrimination. My intention here, in this brief excursion into homosexual thinking, is to stimulate some ideas about gender discrimination. Also to make the connection that gender discrimination against any segment of society perpetuates discrimination for us all. Just as choosing to be "gay" is preference – choice, so is choosing to persecute or discriminate against gays – choice. We also choose to discriminate against women. By definition discrimination is a choice.

Chapter Four

Female Characteristics

FEMALE CHARACTERISTICS

The most salient fact about women is that they bring forth new life: babies. The ability to have children requires a disposition to support and sacrifice for offspring. The role of a mother is to nurture, protect and guide a child towards self-sufficiency. The mother's nurturing role is woven into the psyche of most women; whether or not they have children. Having babies or the potential for doing so creates an "other-centered consciousness" in women.

The ability to have a baby is ordinary in the sense that it is a common experience among women, but actually producing a baby is a physically and psychologically profound event. It is extraordinary in that it creates an other-centered consciousness or ability to think and feel for another being. A mother moves, thinks and feels with her baby before it is born; they are united. Mother and child are literally one being during pregnancy. If a pregnant woman is upset, so is the fetus, and vice versa.

Men cannot share nor even fully understand that psychological experience. They do not "grok" a baby because they cannot have one.

All people participate in a mother-child bonding because we are all born, but only females are capable of directly participating two or more times in mother-child bonding.

After a baby is born the psychological bond expands in a woman in order to embrace all the demands and aspirations a mother has for her child. Biology and society compel women to think and feel for their babies. For a mother it is also natural to think and feel for other children, and then for other people. Women produce children, and from their own experience they develop empathy which is necessary for the guidance of children. From gestating and growing with a baby comes love, the glue that holds society together. Having a baby is quite an ordinary event with extraordinary consequences. Something mystical is born when a mother has a child; a bond more powerful than the sum of its parts.

Mother consciousness is divine in origin (assumption: 3282.9) and speaks to the deepest spiritual aspiration of our species. Other-people consciousness is a pervasive characteristic of females and is usually called maternal instinct. The phrase "mother consciousness" relates the volition of the mind with mothering. A mother's love is so strong; she would sacrifice herself for her child without hesitation. Love at this level is a divine creation.

When a child is born it is engulfed in love, a mystical gift channeled through the mother. The gift of love flows through the mother and is passed on to succeeding generations. Mother Nature conditions all mothers with a desire to love. A baby is a conduit to the well spring of love. Mother love is the fountainhead of all love, and love gives meaning to everything we value. Life is pointless without love. Love is the wellspring from which all civilization is born.

A number of behavior characteristics support and are derived from mother consciousness. One is the female inclination to avoid physical confrontations. Most women have taken the prudent position that it is not advantageous to fight with anyone. It is not fun, safe, or smart and it does not improve the quality of life. If they are in conflict with another person or group, they will try as many alternatives as possible before they will resort to physically fighting. Women will fight if they are compelled to. Threaten a woman's child, and she will fight.

If a woman is going to fight she requires a good reason. Why? In mother consciousness it is a matter of practicality to keep the physical body in good condition; to be able to care for someone else. It is based on the concept: take care of yourself so you can take care of others? There is something very selfish about the male willingness to risk well-being by fighting. Not only are individual combatants putting themselves at risk in a

fight, but the people who are dependent on them are also at risk. Mother consciousness does not want to fight because it has a more compelling function: to nurture. Females have learned by experience that nurturing and fighting are not compatible with one another. They are geared by the mechanics of motherhood to embrace love as a mindset, unite with and embrace others.

Fighting something or someone requires dichotomizing the circumstance so that the opponent becomes an impersonal object. Anger and violence creates an abstract barrier between opposing forces. It is very hard to love your opponent and kill it at the same time.

Violence - Rule of Thumb

The potential for male violence towards women is everywhere, in society, and in every culture. Violence against women is part of the Western world's religious, historical, and legal heritage. Under English common law, a husband had the right to beat his wife, subject to the Rule of Thumb. The Rule of Thumb required him not to use a stick any wider than his thumb. The Rule of Thumb in our common law and language speaks volumes about men and society. There is a quick leap from the Rule of Thumb in our thinking to "Might makes right". That still has an effect on our collective conscious today. Men in western civilization are still influenced by institutions formed long ago which built societies based in part on the belief that women needed to be protected and controlled like property. Men are still encouraged to dominate, control and take charge of women. That can lead to violence when men perceive threats to their property or control.

Because women are on the losing end of most violent situations, they gain a considerable distaste for physical violence and seek alternatives. This alternative trait is a great asset because optional thinking is flexible, resilient and resourceful. The fact is, that females are more adaptable than

males in conflict situations. Adaptation includes creative ways of avoidance and compromise. Most females can sense violence coming a mile off. It compels them to think in terms of redirection. Almost all females, in all societies, must learn as children to circumvent aggressive, violent behavior. Circumventing violence is an ability that is integral to the sociological programming of being a female.

Women as life givers are associated with the blood of creation. Men as life takers are associated with the blood of the hunt and warfare. Women are not typically violent thinkers. Women almost never rape other people, and their crimes of violence and force are statistically minuscule compared to men's. Women represent 11% of the total prison population in the United States, and of this percentage only 4% represents crimes of violence. Criminal behavior is antisocial and inconsistent with a caring, nurturing point of view. To commit a violent crime, a person must first say "I am going to take advantage of someone else, or I am willing to hurt someone". One must think it is OK to hurt someone. Women tend not to think this way. A female is programmed by long tradition to have empathy. Men, usually do not have as much empathy built in; they must acquire it electively.

How we love ourselves, others and the environment will greatly impact human physical evolution and Earth's physical progression and equilibrium. We will progress as a species to the extent that we grapple and understand the principle of love. The love instinct is embedded in all of us – male and female alike. However, women are the progenitors of this force and the keepers of the flame. Men will more easily stray from the guidance of a loving vision. The male agenda: hunting, defending, controlling, conquering, is more inclined to conflict with a love instinct. A man does these "things" because he can.

We are at a crossroad in human evolution. Violence has become more of a burden to humanity than a tool for survival. The primitive male characteristic of using brute force and killing to conquer is putting us all in jeopardy. It is our job as a species to stop destroying each other. It is also our job to stop destroying the Earth. In this regard, the $64,000 questions are the following: Will humans outgrow their need for violence? Will men stop being violent? Will we stop poisoning our nest? Unfortunately there is no clear evidence that this will occur anytime soon, if ever. Warfare and hunting have certainly changed for most men in the world today, and personal violence is all around us. Our ability to be violent has never been greater. That is our problem.

Physical violence towards individuals, nations and the Earth cultures our mindset towards destroying ourselves. Violence grows from the principle of might makes right. It represents one of the two golden rules. The first is "He who holds the gold, makes the rules." This is a variation on the same theme of might makes right. The good thing that happens because of this threat of violence is that some of us become more sensitive and adaptive. Excessive violence and abuse is obviously bad. Some of us stand up and say we want the other golden rule, "Treat people how you would like to be treated." The potential for disaster is great, but so is our growing awareness of what really matters. We need a greater sensitivity in the world of politics, religion and business today. We need to see how foolish our violent direction is.

The ability to compromise easily and see an alternate path is the female forte. Does this mean that females are spineless, without standards? Absolutely not! It means women are guided by the nurturing principle and able to accommodate the unexpected needs of children of all ages. A loving mind has a willingness to flex. The reason is, that females want to make love not war. Women want an environment where babies can flourish. We can complain all day long about the inequities, but it is time to utilize the female assets of conciliation, compassion and compromise. Females have flexibility and desire to have peace. We must use it to our advantage to eliminate the inequity caused by male violence and domination.

Females have acquired a great strength from being subordinate. Women learn to compromise and adjust because they constantly find themselves in subordinate situations. This subordinate position teaches a great lesson, humility. Women have been humbled by violence and the threat of violence. The institutions that men have created in government, business, law, and religion have humbled women by excluding them. Humility is something that men avoid like the plague. Humility and domination are like fire and water. Nobody likes being humbled, but women come to terms with it because they have been forced to do so. Men have literally beaten women into submission.

The humble experience is a great teacher; from it comes greater compassion and empathy. This is a major contributing factor in the formation of mother consciousness. The opposite is also true that one loses compassion and empathy in dominating others. Jesus must have had women in mind when he said, "The meek shall inherit the earth." It takes a great deal of composure and inner strength to submit to an unjust force. The forceful brute is ignorant of the feelings of others because he is unaware of, or chooses not to see, his own frailty.

A humble person knows how others feel because she or he has experienced insecurity. Insecurity is a magnifier of emotions associated with pain. A person who experiences emotional pain yearns for understanding and relief from others. Emotion is the common denominator and the link humans have with each other. It is how we touch each other and ourselves. Emotion gives substance to life.

Mother consciousness grows from association with a baby to larger and larger circles of influence beyond the baby. Mother consciousness is the beginning of a unifying and expanding bond that grows to include family, community, nation, species, planet, and what lies beyond. The mother wants her baby to grow up and go off into a good place – a good world. This is Mother Consciousness. Having "the other" as part of the self is a great gift that is divinely inspired. Mother

consciousness is the perfect metaphor for and a parallel reflection of God consciousness. By definition an omniscient being knows all. Part of our concept of God is that God is a part of us. God sees through our eyes and knows our hearts. We all come from mothers. Most religions allude to the idea that humans come from God, that we are God's children. The first religions were based on the Great Cosmic Mother. The giving of life, a mother function, comes from Mother God, in the same spirit it comes from human mothers. Motherhood is a creative function. This property gives females a powerful base from which to feel their spirituality, a connection with the life-giving divine, the creating function. Females are more advanced than males in being able to project themselves and identify with others because they are mothers or potential mothers. However, a woman must sacrifice a lot to become a mother. Motherhood makes a woman physically vulnerable and psychologically her life becomes much more complicated and difficult.

Thinking and planning for two or more people is much harder than for one and involves increased economic and social responsibility. Women do not have babies because it makes life easier; they have babies because it makes life fuller and more complete. Mother consciousness is an elevated form of selfishness that includes others in its own vision. Biological compulsion has influenced women over thousands of generations to be psychologically willing to accept the burden of babies.

Knowing the other - brings the heart (emotions) into the head (reason). Female thinking, much more so than male, is infused with emotions, intuition and feelings. To be a mother is to be uncertain, vulnerable and fragile; but also, most importantly, courageous. A child is a collection of possibilities that may or may not combine into a desirable sum. A mother knows there will be ups and downs and storms aplenty. A mother accepts the insecurity of life and child rearing and moves forward. The female mind is insecure and knows it - this

is a great strength. The male mind is also insecure; but denies it – this is a great weakness. Children are constantly creating insecurity for themselves and others. Mothers are perpetually dealing with it. The female mind swims in a sea of insecurity and flourishes. Knowing that life is fragile and accepting its insecurity is one of the sweetest characteristics of the female intellect.

Archetypal male thinking is concerned more with strength as a guiding principle: "Be strong, be a man." A man tries to block emotion out of his thinking at first because he thinks it interferes with strength and his vision of life. What a mistake! A man will be compassionate if it supports his image of strength and dominance, but more often than not a man sees emotion and feelings as liabilities that shackle his power. The archetypal female is strong in order to be compassionate. The difference is motivation. Females view strength as an adjunct to emotion, something that assists in knowing and protecting the other. Men utilize strength in their thinking in order to dominate the other. Feelings are inherently more developed in females because they must use them to protect their children. A man blocks or ignores emotion because he thinks it makes him weak. Men try not to feel as much for others because they do not want the "limitations" that compassion dictates.

Menstruation

Another aspect of biology, which puts women in touch with emotions, is the menstrual cycle. The menstrual cycle is a built-in clock constantly ticking and reminding women of their biological nature. Women are forced to pay attention to the rhythms of their bodies and the emotions the menstrual cycle brings. The rhythm of menstruation provides a series of interconnected messages. The body aches and bloating may be perceived as a negative side of an equation or a part of a total bundle of female power. During their menstrual cycle women receives mixed messages. First, they are reminded they are the child bearers, keepers of the human flame. Second, they receive the message that they are either pregnant or not. Menstruation is a whispering thread that all women share – past, present and future. Menstruation connects women to each other and also to the ticking universe. It is a mostly silent and/or sometime-shared bond that is very profound, personal, and yet pervasive. Menstruation speaks to humanity's hopes and fears. Many a man has winced from the remark "I missed my period this month." On the other hand, it ties women together in a very grounded, earthy way.

Menstruation is both a burden and a blessing repeated month after month from childhood to late middle age. Menstruation is charged with strong emotions, disappointment, joy and expectation. It is something that all women share, almost like a collective consciousness or awareness. It is a very private experience that defines being female, being capable of having babies. Although the experience is private, the menstrual cycle strikes a shared resonance and understanding in all women. Almost all women can empathize with another woman if she says, "My period is coming, and I don't feel too good." If a person says "I don't feel too good because I have to see an IRS auditor today," we can all commiserate. However, the cause of the distress is external and not gender-specific. As the song says, "only women bleed". Men do not understand menstruation, but they can observe that it has a profound effect on all women and since it affects them, all people.

Most women acknowledge the phenomenon of menstrual synchronizing. Women living together or in close communication tend to menstruate at the same time. Not all women experience this event, but most agree that it does occur. This phenomenon, menstrual synchronizing, strongly suggests an individual volition over the biological process. The volition is a desire to be in synch with one or more females - a menstrual empathy. It means woman can to some degree alter or control their menstrual cycle.

The volition associated with menstrual synchronizing establishes a logical link, a causation, between the menstrual cycle and the development of human intelligence. Menstrual synchronizing demonstrates a bond between the external world and the internal world in conjunction with volition. In the animal kingdom the estrus cycle is the rule and there is much less volition. With the estrus cycle animals perform biologically. An animal in heat has sex with any mate that shows up. Decision making and volition is very limited. With a menstrual cycle, volition is brought into the equation of biology and consciousness to a much greater extent. Having sex is a conscious decision for those with a menstrual cycle.

There is also evidence of the menstrual process being in synch with the lunar cycle. The interaction may be bi-directional. Perhaps women function in coordination with the moon as does the lunar tide. The idea of menstrual volition has a lot to say about human potential in controlling or influencing the bleeding process, conception, and a whole host of biological functions now thought to be autonomic. Menstrual volition could further lead the way in the development of a human ability to control aspects of autonomic biology. In the same regard that menstrual volition played an important role in the development of consciousness. We have not played this card out yet! Women have much more to discover and teach us all in this regard.

The scientific and philosophical communities are converging with ideas about us taking more control in our own biological and psychological evolution. The time has come for us to take a more proactive role in the process of human evolution. What boundaries we can break or barriers we can breach is stimulating a great debate in society today. The conservative, fearful intellect that we hear arguing against genetic research will be swept away by bold scientists who will ignore religious and legislative regulation. We are on a journey and "the Gods" have given us a Promethean fire in the name of genetic engineering and biofeedback technique. We cannot ignore or lay these tools down. We will use them for good or perhaps ill; but we will use them. The more we realize that what we think, is defining the process of how we think; the more we can synchronize the "what and how" process. We need to learn a great deal more about menstruation and volition. We are not even infants in the universe; we are embryos.

Men do not have any comparable biological experience that defines and bonds them together as a group. Menstruation is a rhythm that clocks women's existence wave after wave, month after month. For women menstruating is like breathing but on a monthly scale; it is the pulsating beat of female existence. It gives women a unique perspective of time that is more of a readiness than a number on a clock. Women perceive time from the inside out; whereas, men are much the opposite. A woman of childbearing age knows each month that goes by from internal signals. Men's awareness of time comes more from external signals of climate, calendars and clock changes. Both males and females have biological rhythms and clocks, but the female clock ticks louder. Men have biological clocks, but they do not hear them. Perhaps they do not listen in the right place or do not listen well in this regard. The universe has repetitive processes with which women are more in tune. The male mind seems more contrived by imposing clocks and calendars on the world. The female mind is more in synch with the repetition and pulse of the universe. Menstruation is an internal cyclical process; whereas a calendar is a mechanical overlay. Males don't feel anything of a comparative nature.

A flower blooms because it is ready, and most of us go to work because it is 8:00 am on Monday morning. Both represent time, but from different perspectives. Women hear and respond to electronic time and pressure too, but they are also compelled to pay attention to their menstrual mechanics. The menstrual clock gives women another dimension to understand time and life. Men do not have, or more correctly, do not choose to acknowledge and pay attention to their bio-clocks. Women feel their bio-clocks but cannot really share them.

Women also have greater physical demarcations in their lives than do men. At each stage of life biological changes are more significant for women: puberty and menstruation, the development of breasts, pregnancy, childbearing and menopause. In contrast at puberty males mostly notice voice change, hair growth and ejaculation. This is not as profound a change as growing breasts and bleeding. The experiences of puberty for males are minuscule in comparison to what female's experience. Males do not have anything comparable to pregnancy or menopause in their lives.

A transfer of training comes from all the changes that occur in the female mind and body. Women learn that adaptation and transformation are psychological as well as physical; women learn to change their point of view along with the shape of their bodies. To be a woman is to understand metamorphosis. Being pregnant is similar to the stage a chrysalis undergoes. The woman's abdomen is like a cocoon, and the birth of a child is like the birth of a butterfly.

Women are more willing to consider emotional problems because their world is more emotionally charged. Females are in touch with physical changes that have strong emotional overtones. To be female is to be emotional. It is women more often than not who seek psychological counseling. It is women who represent the majority of patients in mental hospitals. It comes down to the expression of feelings and emotions: female are more willing to express themselves, and to be at risk for having their expressions aired.

Men have as much capacity for emotion and feelings as women but try much harder to block, ignore, or detach themselves from the experience. For men it is a sign of weakness and an unnecessary source of pain. Feelings create a sense of insecurity for men because they view them as loose cannons on the ship of decision-making. Feelings get in they way of action. Primal man does not want to think about his foe, or the animal he is going to vanquish or feast on. The primal warrior/hunter wants action, not contemplation and

compassion. The problem today is that the nature of hunting and warfare has changed, and the male psychological disposition has not. Modern man is no longer a hunter or a warrior but cannot stop thinking of himself in this mode. Modern man is finding it difficult to adapt primal instincts in a world in which behavior does not need to be primal or violent. This is our Primal Dilemma.

Whether we talk about personal relationships, jobs, religion, or laws, women take a back seat to men. Women are subservient to men. Sometimes it is an unwritten law, but many times it is explicitly written. This programming starts at birth and never ends in our society. Women as well as men participate in the programming of weak women and strong men. Many accept the logic of male domination and approve the practice. However, there are those who see the effects of weak women in society and how it weakens them personally. They recognize the need to stop it.

At first glance the physical and sexual domination of a female mate seems appealing to a man. A sexual slave has a certain animal appeal, but after a nanosecond or two the appeal reveals itself as shallow. If one really analyzes the dynamics of gender domination it does not seem so appealing. For example, if my closest ally, my mate, is reluctant to fight in a situation that confronts one or both of us, I will probably have to fight alone. There is no question that if my mate felt capable of combat I would be a much more formidable enemy. I am not arguing for more combativeness, but for the logic of empowerment. An empowered mate will make me a stronger man and give us both a psychological advantage. A mutually supportive relationship makes us collectively stronger and more viable economically. A more sexually expressive mate will increase the pleasure of all parties. A woman paid equally with men is a greater asset to everybody. A person with confidence in her step is much more pleasurable to walk with than one who is downtrodden.

The issue is psychological empowerment. If we spend energy limiting one another, we weaken ourselves in the process. We can be stronger, richer and smarter than others, but if we support our allies and allow them free expression and empowerment, chances are very good we will all benefit. The male/female experience is analogous to a man walking around holding a hand over one eye. If he were to release the hand, not only would full vision be restored, but he would gain the use of another hand. There is no real advantage to keeping anyone in a subservient position. Discrimination is a form of imprisonment. What we all must realize is that when we chain someone down, we are also tethered to that chain.

passive/aggressive

Most women give their power away in relationships with men. Women have been conditioned and intimidated for so long that they defer automatically, almost constantly to men. Women at work or at home underplay the power of their role in relation to men. Women frequently play a game with men in relation to power. It is called passive/aggressive behavior. Women will defer to men, but they don't like it. They say to themselves, "Yes, your are my boss; or you are physically stronger; or you have the upper hand in this situation, but I don't like it". Who, really, likes being dominated? No one! Passive/aggressive behavior is retaliatory. Passive/aggressive behavior is a way of getting back at someone because one doesn't want to be open about retaliation. At times women will resort to the passive/aggressive behavior of refusing to have sex when they feel too much is demanded of them. It's difficult for a man to understand it. The man says: "I come home from working all day, and all I expect is that you take care of the kids, mow the lawn, do the laundry, wash the dishes, make dinner and desert, clean the yard, clean the house, mend my socks, don't spend money, decorate the house and ……

and…..and…. and now at the end of the day all I want is a little sex. How come you have a headache?"

Over the centuries women have developed many passive/aggressive responses to the male/female interaction. Passive aggression is a sour grapes activity in response to a dominating person or institution. It is a protest, but it is not quite out front or revealing. It is behavior that is designed to influence or punish in a somewhat covert manner, and it is related to someone else's action. Passive aggression is angry and reactionary behavior. It can be conscious or subliminal, or both on the part of the perpetrator. It is intended to annoy or punish someone about whom we feel powerless. Passive aggression is an adaptation of those who are outside the ring of power who feel unable to exert their influence directly. All of us employ passive/aggressive behavior at one time or another. For example, you turn your cell phone off when you know someone wants to get a hold of you.

If one is held in a position of perpetual powerlessness, there is a natural tendency to feel resentful. Resentment is the key to understanding passive aggression. If power is denied a person for any reason, gender, color, ethnicity or whatever, animosity and resentment are understandable. It does not matter if the reasons are justified or not. Passive aggression is about lack of power and resentment – not righteousness.

In male/female relationships, power disparity and resentment abound. Therefore, it should be no surprise that women employ passive/aggressive behavior very frequently. As noted earlier women are the gatekeepers of sexuality. The realm of sex is very powerful. Any woman is capable of withholding sex in a passive/aggressive dynamic. The very nature of our calculating intellects compels us, sometimes, to use a powerful circumstance to our perceived advantage. Our challenge is to understand and outgrow behavior that does not serve us or our world. We all participate and have a role in passive/aggression; we all have to work together to overcome this behavior when it hurts us more than it helps us.

When an individual is held powerless, corollary issues of self-esteem come into play. Low self-esteem usually works hand in hand with passive aggression. Part of the person acknowledges and accepts the position of powerlessness, but another part protests the condition. For example, if a husband makes disparaging remarks about his wife's intelligence, she may respond by making his coffee deliberately too strong or sweet. Some part of her says, "I may not be as smart as you are, but I have the power to punish you." That perpetrator has accepted a deficit - real or imagined - and a position of less power. When one commits passive/aggressive behavior, it is like signing a contract. First, one accepts a position of less power. Second, one states that they don't like it. Third, they devise a plan to punish the other person or institution. This conditions an individual to partially accept a judgment and low self-esteem in the process. Low self esteem becomes part of the contract.

If you can acknowledge an insensitive remark, you are not diminished or changed one bit. You are still the same person before and after the remark. If we really discuss your remark, it will probably reveal your feelings of insecurity and uncertainty. It is important to realize that passive/aggressive behavior does give us a degree of satisfaction, but it also helps to keep us in a position of weakness because it partially acknowledges and accepts the real or alleged weakness. Passive/aggressive behavior protests a perceived or real inequity but usually seeks not resolution but revenge; therefore, the scenario is repeated and the weakness lives on.

Passive/aggressive behavior is hard to change because it does give a certain satisfaction. "Secret revenge is double sweet." Female domination by males is rooted in the superior physical strength of males. This strength condition will not change, but male/female domination can. We have been on the road of equalization for quite some time. Part of the process of equalization and growth involves recognition of the detrimental aspects of passive aggression.

Passive/aggression is both good and bad, useful and harmful. It can be used to a beneficial end in the feminist movement as political votes. This is not to say that feminist votes are passive/aggressive in nature. Each vote has its own motivation and reasons for being. But all voting can be by its very nature to some degree a passive/aggressive reaction because it is or can be secret. Voting is a silent protest against a Goliath. We all sling our stones (votes) in a hope that positive change will occur and injustice punished. As proponents of change we must use all sources of power to our advantage. We must encourage a vote of change for female political candidates.

The cycle of male domination is definitely beginning to change. Awareness of the problem is growing, and this is the first step in the process of change. Both men and women must become increasingly aware of the problem of male domination and how it is connected to other human issues that retard our development. Recognition that women are deprived of equal participation when there is equal capacity is the foundation of feminism and WouldArt.

Someone once said, "Every job should be open to everyone unless it actually requires a vagina or a penis." Recognition or awareness of "the problem" can take many forms and levels of understanding. Some people can only understand discrimination as it relates to them personally. Some people see the inequities but do not care because they think it does not affect them. Many people are apprecilative of feminist issues but do not know how to act appropriately or feel powerless to act. All of the above make up the great majority of people in the United States and throughout the world.

The onus for WouldArt leaders is to extract some response, however small, from a substantial amount of people. The response that works best for public issues is the vote.

The next vital step after awareness is to take some empowering action, be it ever so small. No point of view or thought has any substance until some behavior is manifested from it. Voting is a very empowering action. Women must take the lead in bringing the feminist agenda to the political table and a vote. More attention must be focused on issues and candidates who will address feminist concerns.

Humility and Compassion

Many times females find themselves in vulnerable or weak positions or circumstances. A psychological vulnerability develops because they feel physically or psychologically threatened. The psychological feeds off of the physical vulnerability and vice versa. Women have learned something very positive from those negative circumstances, humility and compassion. Conversely there are many stories of males who became ruthless and dictatorial because they invest a lot of their energy in being physically and psychotically dominant. There is something to be said for winning or being king of the heap. Dominant and submissive people and circumstances will always exist, but we have to strive to balance ourselves and be aware of what we manifest in the world as well as in ourselves. An integrated person strives to balance these attributes. The most advanced human is one who uses both the heart and head in decision-making. Both sexes must continue to learn and take from each other in the thinking, decision-making process. Males and females are on separate highways trying to find each other. We need better road maps to find, understand and appreciate one another. Infusing strength with compassion is the job of both sexes. Clearly this idea is central to the equal participation of women in world affairs.

Women are not superior or inferior to men; they are different. A lot of emphasis is placed on the comparison of men and women in the tasks they do, or would like to do, or what they perceive they can do. Life should not be a contest where we beat the opposition, where everything that is not like us, is against us. Ideally life should be a process in which we learn to progress and live with all things around us. The idea that women are weak is as corrupt as the thought that women are better than men. Men and women are on a journey, together whether they like it or not. Our job is to coexist and co-control our selves and manage the environment. Women are not better than men. Men are not better than women. We are different in many ways, and we are alike in many ways. The competitive attitude fosters a sense of alienation and separation of the sexes. Whether or not a man or woman can do a particular job is not the issue. We are companion travelers on a journey. Our journeys are all individual but make up the collective journey of humankind. If we are to continue our journey collectively, we must understand our personal relationships with people, plants and animals. Nothing is unrelated.

BIRTH CONTROL

More than anything else in recent history, reliable birth control is responsible for the burgeoning of the feminist movement. It was not until women were physically and psychologically freed from the consequences of sex, pregnancy, that they could entertain freedom and equality in all aspects of life. The Pill prevented the male seed from fertilizing the egg, but it acted like a seed in fertile ground in the minds of women around the world. It gave women time and space to think about who they are and where they want to go. Before reliable contraception, women were prisoners of their own biology in relation to sex and pregnancy. Birth control has been around for thousands of years, but until recent times it has not been reliable. Without reliable birth control, pregnancy is an aspect of a woman's life out of her control. Birth control allowed women the ability to plan not only children but life courses as well. It opened up doors of thinking and possibilities for all of humankind.

Women have made more advances in independence, freedom and power in the last forty or fifty years than in the proceeding four or five thousand years. This is not to say the battle has been won. We have a long way to go. The logical extension of woman's liberation is freedom of choice for all people, men and women. Woman's freedom is key to human freedom. Effective birth control provided a great passageway for female development. Birth control in itself does nothing for anybody. It does not alter a person, but it provides options and possibilities. The power of birth control is that it gives people time to consider alternatives in their lives.

In 1848, Elizabeth Cady Stanton and Lucretia Mott convened a conference at Seneca Falls, New York for the adoption of the Declaration of Sentiments, which was intended as a Declaration of Independence for Women. At that time Cady Stanton talked to a reporter and said "Self-development is a higher responsibility than self-sacrifice. The thing that most retards and mitigates against women's self-development is self-sacrifice."[3]

That is a true and profound revelation. The more one sacrifices for childcare and family support, the less resources and energy remain for self-development. Undeveloped women are dependent upon males for sustenance. Birth control is directly related to self-development, which is predicated upon the ability to control one's direction in life. If most of my energy is consumed by children and associated tasks, I cannot otherwise develop. If I can postpone having children until I am ready at 30, 35 or 40; I can focus my energy on myself and my own development.

Patriarchal society wants women to be self-sacrificing. If the woman will take care of the children and the house, the man can develop himself in order to support the family. This is the formula for most families in the world. The formula makes it very difficult for women to self-develop. The birth of children becomes a matter and means of the control of women. It is birth control in reverse; by birthing women are controlled!

---

[3] http://plato.stanford.edu/entries/feminism-ethics/

Abortion is another control issue in relation to women's freedom or degree of liberty. The heart of the issue is self-sacrifice versus self-development. Not having the option to abort a fetus limits personal power. This is a clear example of how personal power is related to political power. Patriarchal society restricts abortion, and in so doing limits women's access to power, both personal and political. Obviously from women's political point of view it is beneficial to have abortion legal. Whether or not it is morally correct to abort a fetus is another concern entirely. A joke I heard addresses this issue. Like many jokes, it is simultaneously silly and profound: "It is not whether you win or lose but where you go after the game." In this regard the game is self-development and self-sacrifice in relation to birth control and abortion.

If we were really to give in to the anti-abortion and anti-birth control movements, where would this game take us? At what point in overpopulation do we start to kill people by design? We have six billion people now; early in my life, not long ago, there were only three billion on Earth. People in many nations are starving now; what will happen when there will be 10 or 15 billion people? It is possible that in fifty years there could be 50 billion people on this planet. Is the issue really life, or is it death? So much of the talk in the anti-abortion circles is about preserving a life, saving a soul. However, the main issue for these people is preventing death.

Death is the true test of faith and the thing most feared by people. We live by death, by killing other entities, and yet we fear death as something unnatural or unnecessary. We all want to be immortal, and we hope and pray that immortality exists because we are afraid of death as a dead end. In most religious teachings we try to convince each other that we are on a path to immortality. Most of us go through life not thinking about our own deaths, but the deaths of others. We tell each other stories and fables about how we will live forever in various versions of wonderland.

The fact is that death is the basis for life, but we don't like it. In our heart of hearts we are not sure if we are part of immortality. Life is insecure and death fills us with uncertainty. Save a fetus; prevent a death; prevent our own death; gain a brownie point; go to heaven. Is this an accidental design or is life insecure on purpose? I am not advocating brutality but sensibility. At every stage of life we are given practical choices. If we choose impractical alternatives, they usually accumulate and culminate in tragedy. Not controlling the population of the Earth is suicidal and will bring us sooner than later to global catastrophe. The population of this Earth cannot keep growing if all our needs are met. As time goes on we must regulate the right to birth more and more on this planet. The Wild Wild West of babies unlimited is over, or at least it should be over. We are reaching the point where there is nowhere to expand. We are centuries, and maybe thousands of years away from being technologically able to colonize other habitable planets. We will either control our birth rate voluntarily or the death rate will be controlled by warfare, plagues and/or environmental disaster. We live in a finite house – how many people do you want in your house?

Chapter five

Men and Women

Men and Women

Men and women have many different skill sets, but their ability to reason and formulate ideas and solutions are on par with each other. For sure they employ a different mindset in the formulating and solving of certain types of problems. There is a difference, and this is a good thing. Science has not revealed a substantial difference in the cognitive abilities of the sexes. Women are as capable as men in doing most jobs. There are some jobs that require large amount of brute force that women do not do as well, but most jobs don't require a lot of force - they require brains. And there are some jobs that require a small and delicate touch that women are better suited for. Realistically there is very little that must be done by a woman or a man exclusively. When women join male dominated occupations they perform as well. Although opportunities are improving for women, they still face discrimination in the workplace. Women have a much harder time rising to the top ranks in male dominated professions. The fact remains that men control the reigns of power in most professions and do not easily let them go.

Why have men assumed control of the leadership positions in philosophy, religion, government and science? Easy answer - because they could. There is no better explanation. Men are the physical protectors, guardians of society – our warriors. Men are still exclusively the guardians of "society" because of the transference of authority from the warrior status which never included women.

There is a very short step from being physically dominant to being psychologically dominant. Physical intimidation also includes psychological intimidation. This intimidation permits domination in the world of ideas. A physical protector that morphs into a psychological protector is like a fox in charge of the chicken coop. Are men smarter than women? Is male philosophy better than female

philosophy? Of course not, but historically, most philosophy, until recently, has been written by men. This is an extremely important and revealing statistic! Philosophy is the basis for a society's system of beliefs, ethics and authority. Again, men have made the rules and set up society's institutions, thereby ensuring perpetual positions of leadership and power for themselves.

Military might, economic power, control of natural and technological resources, all of these forces are coordinated under the banner of government. Philosophy shapes religion which in turn shapes government. Government creates laws and regulations. There is a causal relationship between philosophy and all institutions – especially government. Simply put, philosophy, a common, agreed upon set of beliefs, rules the world.

The divine

It is extremely important that we explore and question our religious beliefs. One can make the metaphor that analysis of beliefs is equivalent to owning your house. If someone else does the thinking and you accept that thinking; then you are just renting the beliefs. Own your beliefs, don't be a renter. The way to own a belief or idea is to thoroughly examine it.

In this regard it is helpful to take various angles or approaches in considering the divine. Sometimes it is beneficial to think outside the box, in order to get a better perspective. Here are some questions, to help start the process.
1. What if we come in contact with the real creator of this universe and it refuses to be our God?
2. What if it doesn't want worship?
3. What if it only wants to be our friend?

4. What if this creator doesn't like us and what we have done with ourselves and the planet?
5. What if it just doesn't care one way or the other about us?
6. What if we are like fleas to our creator or worse, defective and diseased?
7. What if our creator is not divine at all?
8. What if our creator is malevolent?
9. What if our creator is defective in our eyes?

We could be looking at layers in the hierarchy of nature and creation. We may have been created by something that is not omnipotent. It may have been created by something of a higher order but still not divine. What are we to the monkey, frog, ant, or ameba? Do we want to be Gods, have the responsibility of stewardship for these creations? The answer is probably both yes and no. A part of us would like to be all powerful and knowing but another part is fearful of what we do. There may be an infinite number of infinite universes. There may be an infinite number of possibilities that create life, each more powerful than the next. Maybe none of these creators is omnipotent. There may be no such thing as omnipotence. Isn't it possible that we as humans are in a small tributary of a gigantic river of creators who are progressively more powerful than the last? Perhaps none of them is omnipotent?

Many people think we are the only beings in this universe. What will we think of ourselves if we contact other beings from other worlds? Can we easily explain to the aliens that women are not man's equal? What if they are one million years more advanced in their civilization than ours? Would we try and lecture them and tell them that it is God's will that women be kept down? What if they are asexual? What if they are infinitely more powerful than us? Will they become our new God or Gods? How do we justify our

behavior towards women to a superior species? Is it possible that we are not aware of all the dimensions around us?

These questions can help move our boundaries. Spiritual thinking is important for all of us. We all pay heed to it. Our thinking can very easily get stale. We need a flexible mind to create new ideas in order to change the way the world works. If women are to be recognized as equal leaders and builders of society; religion must change. Religion is at the base of society's institutions. If we want to change power structures in our society; religion will have to change with it.

Insecurity

Insecurity is integral to consciousness. Descartes' maxim "I think, therefore I am," points to the fact that we are always trying to define ourselves and know who we are. We struggle at every stage of life to define ourselves. This also means we do not know or are not certain at any given time who we are. We are becoming.

Artists are on the cutting edge of insecurity. They are trying to construct that which has never existed before. They are trying to define reality in new ways. Scientists are in a similar condition trying to figure out how the world works. What's the saying "the more you know, the more you find out what you do not know." Theologians and philosophers are also dealing with insecurity on a very primal level. By asking the questions like: "what is the purpose of life?"; "what is God?"; "what is good and evil?" Which came first – insecurity or needs? We are always dealing with our sense of insecurity.

We should learn from dinosaurs that our presence on earth is not guaranteed. Life is fragile. We learn from the natural world by observation. By observing ecosystems we learn about the harmony and destruction of our world. Studying symbiosis teaches us how interdependent we are with even the smallest microorganisms. When an ecosystem gets out of balance it will come apart. Civilizations are out of balance because men do not nurture properly. Men left totally in charge loose their sense of balance in the stewardship of our institutions.

We must work together if there is going to be a viable future. Women must step in and temper the male perspective. With more effort we can really restore our planet. What would be the characteristics of an ideal world: peace on earth; opportunity and prosperity for women as well as men; conservation of resources; meaningful education and work for all; no crime; freedom to grow and learn? Are these goals attainable? I do not know, but I do know that if you do not have goals you can not go anywhere. There will always be elements among us that will try to sabotage our constructive efforts, but it is advantageous to maintain an optimistic perspective. I take a share of responsibility for the way things are, but I know that I make a difference when I use Earth's resources conservatively and when I yield power to women. I make a difference.

No civilization or institution traverses time unchanged. We must make some fundamental alterations in how we govern ourselves and the world. A big part of that equation, now, is changing how women are treated. The scheme of slavery was zealously defended only 150 years ago. Today we can only imagine how very crude and brutal that arrangement was. I hope one hundred and fifty years in the future people will be looking back from our time as another transition point for the freedom of women.

Because we are aware of who we are, our actions, and thoughts, we also can feel our insecurities. A lot of our motivation comes from this awareness. Insecurity prods us constantly. However, a good deal of the time we do not acknowledge the source and we are not in touch with what is driving us. Knowing that you are insecure is a tremendous asset. Ignoring or hiding from this fact is huge liability. We can then use this knowledge as a motivational tool. We have to stop deceiving ourselves about insecurity. We can use insecurity, both individually and as a group, to motivate and propel us in a more focused direction. The one direction that we must learn about and agree upon is protecting our planet. Religious, economic, political, and social differences mean nothing if we do not have a sustainable place to live and workout whatever it is we believe.

Unfortunately, there is a payoff for both men and women in maintaining a dual class society. Men have placed themselves in a superior position to wield the power of the world. Power for men is used to augment primal insecurity they have in relation to themselves and women. Men feel insecure about their ability to provide for a family which is closely linked to men's ability to attract a mate. Having a mate is necessary for obtaining sex at predictable intervals. Reliable sex drives men to establish power structures which keep them in control. Women benefit from men in power because they think that they are relieved of the daily responsibilities of survival and sustenance. This social hierarchy is on the one hand expedient, but on the other it is harmful. We have developed basic misconceptions about the male/female relationship. We need to reexamine the human dynamic in relation to the earth and our deal with each other.

One of the strategies an insecure person employs, which means anyone of us, is putting someone else down in order to make you feel better. The assumption is that if you go down in stature then I go up. The reality is just the opposite. Look at politicians when they viciously attack one another. What do you think of someone who verbally abuses another? When one physically dominates another (or some group - women, blacks, native Americans, etc.) the abuse of that person does not make one stronger or more powerful but actually weaker. They reveal their own poor character, not to mention their expenditure of negative energy. There is also the loss of power in the fact that one now has an enemy instead of an ally. By dominating or insulting someone we

lose the potential for collaborative effort. As this planet becomes more crowded, collaboration becomes even more imperative.

There are great lessons to be learned from the natural world. One of the most important is to realize that most all species that have ever lived are now extinct. From the point of view of many modern cultures today, particularly patriarchal ones, all Earth's resources exist so that mankind can exploit them to perpetuate our species. Our dilemma now, and for the future, is to reign in those who continue to do harm to our nest. People who are unapologetic in their beliefs that mankind can continue this course in perpetuity are not realists. If we can see anything in Mother Nature it is how fragile and tenuous life is on this planet.

Why do we have so many hero and role model figures in our lives? You know, sports personalities, movie stars, beauty queens, media figures, literary hero's, business tycoons, etc. Why do we look up to a man who can whip ten strong men at one time? Why do we look up to someone who knows all the right questions and seems to have the best answers? It is because we want to be like them. This implies a dissatisfaction with part of ourselves? Heroes are our alter egos. Having a role model is a safe and perhaps constructive way of expressing our insecurity about our own condition. It also acts as a target for us to strive towards. Again, the important point is that our need for heroes illustrate that we have a sense of insecurity.

We are far removed in time from our primate ancestors but nevertheless still possess the primal qualities of males being stronger in stature and physically dominant as compared to females. In our modern times we now can change our individual and collective destinies in dramatic ways. We can mitigate and modify the roles and responsibilities that males and females play in the group. As roles, evolve so does the configuration in which society functions.

The first spiritual leaders in society were priests and priestesses - shaman. They supplied the answers to troubling questions and perplexities. The archeological evidence indicates that in Neolithic society this function was shared by men and women. As males became more proficient in warfare and physical domination they also constructed and assumed control of belief systems of cultures, the psychological/philosophical world. The priest became male only and the authority figure who had answers for the profound question of existence. The priest function is still very important today but a new figure stands beside the priest and dispenses answers - the scientist. The scientist provides theories about the unknown and reaches towards the infinite. The priest offers certitude; the scientist offers theories; both look at the infinite unknown. The scientist speculates and the priest postulates.

Telling women that they can not compete as mathematicians, mechanics, carpenters and engineers is not only untrue but intellectually dishonest. Males promote female weakness because it offsets their profound sense of insecurity. The programming of female inferiority or male superiority starts at birth and never stops. There is a psychological correlation in the male mind between control and security.

This point is very important and closely related to male insecurity as it relates to spirituality. Male dominated theology is in conflict with the observable world. Men envision themselves as masters of the world and have in the western tradition created a male God even though the dominate characteristics of nature are female. The aspects of nature such as birth, ebb & flow, and rebirth are profoundly female characteristics. Men in western theology are trying to control aspects of life which are out of their control; so they create a theology which portrays God as a male and deduce that mortal men are required to control our institutions. Western theology is designed to not only put men in power but to deny reality and women participation in leading institutions.

Some of the most profound truths in the human condition are confusing. For example: in order to posses some one's love you must let them be free to choose. It is also a paradox to realize that you can only get rid of your anger and rage by accepting it. One does not get control of life by demand but by surrendering to the flow. One must lose life or something of value in order to appreciate its worth. Another paradox is that men will become more powerful by accessing their feminine attributes of intuition, nurturing and visible emotions. Typically, in our culture, men do not want to be complemented for having feminine attributes, but think it best to hide them. We must come to terms with these paradoxes and mature as a species. We must blend our soft attributes and abilities with the hard realities of culture and custom.

If you ask a man to define himself he talks first about his job, house, position in society, maybe car and then family and interests last. A women talks about relationships first and then how she looks, how happy or depressed they are. Defining oneself is very revealing.

Continuing with the idea that we exhibit some primal characteristics of our ancestors, another significant trait is the hierarchical/social system we inherited. Men are concerned more with the power of the pecking order and in a larger sense, in the order of community. Women place more energy into building cohesiveness within the group. Males build the vertical structure of the community (hierarchy) and females provide the horizontal structure (cohesiveness). Men control the political, economic, military and spiritual community and women provide the support to sustain and bind all communities together. I once saw a singles ad by a woman in a newspaper which said "you make the living and I make the living worth while".

Primates are primarily vegetarian with a low consumption of fat in their diet. Eating large quantities of meat is related to an increase of aggression. The very process of meat eating is aggressive. For a number of reasons it is to our advantage to modify our eating habits more in line with our primate cousins. It is healthier, more efficient, and perhaps can have a positive effect on how we share and manage our communities.

Not seeing ourselves as a global people is related to the limitations we place on ourselves personally and in relation to gender. Besides striving for and achieving equality for women where we all benefit, we need a global self consciousness. With our focus here we can begin to correct our social and environmental problems. Without it we are stuck in a much smaller circle of understanding and action. If we only take care of only our immediate families we will ruin our communities and concomitantly our planet.

Men have taken on the burden and staked out the territory of explaining the uncertainties of the human condition whether it be through the theoretical world of philosophy, religion or science. This is a tiresome, haunting task. As men, we need to back away from knowing all the answers. As women, we need to step forward with more answers. Together we need to collaborate more and embrace our uncertainty, have the courage to face the future of men and women as equal partners, and admit that life on Earth is tenuous for all of us.

Most people confuse power and money with intelligence and skill. It is assumed that if you are rich or powerful or both that you are smart or smarter than the next person. This is not necessarily so. Most people who are in positions of wealth or power are there because of circumstance or inheritance. There are a few who start with nothing and amass a fortune with a combination of skill, intelligence, timing and sometimes brutality. Having intelligence, sensitivity and insight are not necessarily synonymous with being wealthy. Those that spend their time making money exclusively, usually benefit no one but themselves. It is rare for an individual to have a drive for both money and knowledge and the well being of all humanity.

In our culture we worship money and the people who have it. In our thinking money is a key to unlocking a door to happiness, freedom and dreams. Money also makes us feel insecure. Money is a lever in the toolbox of opportunity and a double edged sword. Money is like wielding a powerful tool, like a chainsaw. You can do great things with a chainsaw, you can also mess things up.

Insecurity is around every corner in our consciousness. The positive aspect is that it propels us forward and drives us to action. It is through a projection of ourselves into the future that we can assist steering a course for humankind now. This is tremendously difficult to do, and has been very elusive so far. We can not agree on where to go or what to do. We are always going someplace but we never seem to get there by concerted effort, we just kind of accidentally arrive places. More and more the places we arrive at are undesirable.

Volition

We need to coordinate our volition in order to change how we think of ourselves individually and as a group. We need to take responsibility for our own evolution. We must also not ignore the obvious; women are one half of the population. Women can contribute one half of the ideas toward our collective system of beliefs and institutions and can contribute one half of our leaders.

It is not possible for us to answer all of the mysteries of the universe. One of the biggest mistakes organized religion makes is not appreciating and letting the unknown exist. Answering questions which are unknowable end up being absurd. Some "things" are just out of our scope of comprehension - grasp. When a religion asserts that God is a male, a person is compelled to either accept this statement, which is the most common choice, or question it. Can God be a insect, woman, asexual non-human or anything it wants? If you were omnipotent would you limit yourself to appear as a man?

Most religions use peer pressure to obtain conformity and compliance with its beliefs. But on the other hand, if organized religions admitted they did not have all the answers to the unknown they might lose their appeal. The objective of religion is to provide answers to quell a troubled mind. Religion has always known that in quieting a mind it also controls it. The job of the church is to provide comfort. In return it receives control and collects a tax

Is it a myth or fact that women have poor math and mechanical skills? If it is a myth that women's skills are deficient; why are not more women mechanics and mathematicians? If it is a fact that women are less capable in math, science and mechanics, how do we explain those who achieve competence? Women's ability in math and mechanics is both myth and fact. It is a myth because many more women can be made capable with the right training and encouragement. It is also a fact that females have not developed math and mechanical skills to the same degree as men because they have lacked opportunity and encouragement. It is hard for young girls who are dominated by assertive boys in math and science classes to excel and become competent. Most girls do not build things because they are not encouraged to. It all comes down to encouragement, training and opportunity. You can have all the natural ability in the world to be something: carpenter, jeweler, cook, etc., but if you do not practice it or something related, you're not going to be very good.

Anything that we do has a strong component of uncertainty associated with it. Love is one of the most

positive of human emotions. But love is packed full of uncertainty. Do we love someone only for love's sake or is there an aspect of fear that we will not be loved back? Human emotions, particularly love, are defined by their opposites. What we admire and value, is defined in part by what we do not admire and value. Can we be happy without knowing what sadness is or vice versa? Of course not, the full range of human emotion is necessary in order for us to have meaningful experiences.

Empathy and Love

A women's strength is that she sees herself as part of the other. She feels for another body because she knows this other body, it came from her. She is a mother - she knows empathy. Most men are struggling to develop their sense of empathy. A man who understood empathy was Gandhi.

Gandhi's power in conflict was that he would take abuse, much like a woman. Gandhi taught the world not with arrogance but with humility. He was a true saint in many ways. Although, Gandhi had a better vision for people globally, than he did in his personal life. Women are not all saints either, but they approach the world much like Gandhi: from a position of weakness that knows it is strong and worthy. Knowing that women contain this special strength affirms the hope that we can make the world for the better for all of us.

The caterpillar transforms itself through a chrysalis to become a butterfly. A caterpillar is a fragile creature. A cocoon is a marvelous house that gives birth to a beautiful butterfly. As a species I would say we are somewhere between the caterpillar and chrysalis stage of development. Hopefully we can make a transformation and become more than we are now. Our potential to evolve for the better is so strong that it would be tragic if we do not. We need to all

Which Came First... Insecurity Or Needs?

begin to understand that consciousness is the major factor in human evolution.

In a similar regard it is important to understand how important components are formed in our consciousness. Let's ask some questions, in order to elicit answers. What is the most powerful day of your life? What is the most important day? Some people say it is the day my child was born; or when they graduated from college. There are a lot of answers to this question. I guess we could question the question and say there is no one day that is more important or powerful. Or is the answer – everyday. Or now is the most important day. However, there is one special day for each and every one of us. The day we were born. I have asked this question a lot recently in conversation and most people remark that they do not remember being born. Very true, no one remembers the day we were born because we are a Tabla Rasa – a blank slate. But, without a doubt, if there were no birth, no subsequent days would exist.

Another question is: what is the most valuable thing you have ever received? The answers to this question vary widely. Some talk about children or monetary gifts or husbands or wives. All valid answers, but are they the most valuable gift? I would say no. The most valuable gift we have ever received is love. Why, because love allows us to grow beyond ourselves and develop predilections to reach the stars. And where does love come from and when do we get it? We receive love before we are born from our mothers. Mothers love their babies because they are one being. Love is a spiritual gift that grows with babies. All of our desires and values are framed from our ability to love. Our likes and dislikes are a reflection of our love.

The origin of our love is another thing that most people have forgotten. Most of us don't give credit to our mothers for our very lives and, more importantly, the ability to love. We have forgotten about it and we take it for granted. However, love, begins in each one of us and comes first from a mother to a child. Love is the basis on which all relationships depend. When I say all relationships I mean: family, community, towns, cities, states, nations, planet and beyond. Love is the glue of human civilization and the basis for all values. You may say that "I love pizza or I love tea", but you don't love anything unless you love yourself. You get and you learn love from your mother first. Mother love paves the way for every other predilection in our lives. Yes, a father shows and gives us love, but a mother gives and teaches love first and best.

    You ever hang around a pregnant woman? All she talks and thinks about is her baby. The bond of love is forged over nine months. I talked to my babies while they were in the uterus and they immediately recognized my voice upon birth. And I showered all the love I could on them after they were born. But I could not compete with the bond my wife had with the babies while in the womb or after with breast feeding. We are loved first and most powerfully by our mothers. Mother love is the spring from which all love flows.

Chapter six

Our Religions

Our Religions

The New Oxford American Dictionary defines philosophy as the study of the fundamental nature of knowledge, reality, and existence. All other sciences came from the science of philosophy. Indeed it was our first science. It was born from our need to address the great unknowns of our universe.

Thinking is the primary activity we do as humans. Critical thinking is what really differentiates us from other animals. We use thinking to build our systems and to deal with our problems. However, thinking is a double-edged sword because it also creates insecurities. Some of the fundamental questions that vex us have been the seeds from which sprang the institution of religion.

Religion as an institution developed before any government and probably before even simple business relationships. The first person to ask a question about the human condition set the stage for the religious exchange. Just imagine a person asking "Where did I come from?" When someone stepped forward with an answer – that was when the institution of religion was born.

Religion is a business because it is based on quid pro quo; you give something and you get something. Religion is a simple business equation - supply and demand. The equation for the religious transaction is quite clear. Religion supplies absolute answers and guidelines for moral behavior. Followers provide allegiance and financial rewards on the other side of the equation. We have a buyer and seller. All evidence and logic suggests Religion has been around for as long as humans have been asking questions. It supplies our need for guidelines for social interaction. It addresses the most basic questions of humankind.

Religious thinking is our defense, the levee that holds back the great flood of disturbing ideas that make us nervous, and unsettle us.

The most basic questions about our existence are not easily answered and are always with us. Can they be answered? That depends on your point of view. It depends on what philosophy (religion) you subscribe to. Philosophy was the first science, and religion was the first institution born from that science. Is religion a science? Some would argue yes, and some no. I would say religion is a science of conjecture. All religions create stories in an attempt to provide guidelines for living. If you are a Hindu, the story of creation is quite different than the Hebrew line of reasoning. And, they can not all be true.

Not everyone has an opinion about baseball or spaghetti but everyone has religious opinions. Even if you don't subscribe to any religion; if you're an atheist or agnostic – that's an opinion – a position. Religion has been around for as long as people have been able to ask, "Who am I"? Religion will always be with us in one form or another because we are not masters of our world. We know very little about our own planet and almost nothing about the greater universe. We cannot easily answer those questions, which a three year old asks such as "Is there a heaven?" We as adult/individuals cannot answer the ultimate questions easily or absolutely. In contrast, every religion ever created offers answers to the three ultimate questions:

1. Who are we?
2. Where do we come from?
3. Where are we going?

There will always be debate and controversy about the nature of our existence. What is not so obvious is the relationship religion has to other institutions in society that are not religious.

Priestesses, Priests and Shaman's

Archeological evidence and logic support the idea: that shamans, priests and priestesses were around at the beginning of civilization. At the dawn of human settlements, evidence shows fertility Goddesses and cave art. A Fertility Goddess was an answer to the question of how we and the universe were created and interact. The creator of cave art and fertility Goddesses was a religious leader.

Cave art is a spiritual explanation for the questions that haunted our first ancestors just as religious icons, texts, and sacraments offer answers to the questions that still plague us today. It demonstrates how important religion and its hierarchy of religious leaders, priestesses, priests, and shamans were, and still are today. We respect our religious leaders because they calm our fears, chase away our demons and guide us in how to live. Religions have set the framework for the nuclear family, what foods we should eat, what jobs we should do; when and with whom we should have sex, etc. It is the authority – the rule maker.

Logic can lead us further to understand our beginnings by asking - "What is the oldest profession"? The answer has always been – prostitute. However, a finger pointer, or condemner had to exist, first, before the prostitute. This moralist was a priest, shaman or religious leader. Logic tells us that the preacher is the "oldest profession" and had to precede the prostitute.

The preacher tells us what is taboo and what is OK. Our religious leaders establish the moral and ethical codes that society uses. Early religious leaders offered reasons for the structure and behavior of the physical and natural world. In essence it, religion, was our first science. Imagine, if you will, a small group of related people huddled around a cave campfire with a lead person grunting out stories about where

the first trees came from and how they grow. It isn't much of a step from that camp fire to an evangelical television program with a preacher expounding on the science of creationism. From the very beginning of communities religious leaders had ideas about creation, moral and ethical codes. When villages formed and businesses started, people appealed to the most trusted thinkers, their religious leaders, to guide them. They helped formulate governments and businesses in the very beginning and they still do today.

The church, i.e., all organized religions; helps formulate the philosophical principles for secular institutions. A direct relationship between the church and a company charter does not always exist, but there is always a causal relationship. Many of the early European settlements in the new world, for example, were church founded and funded enterprises. Today many of the insurance and savings and loan companies began as church enterprises that helped their parishioners.

Most people are a product of their religious heritage. We are programmed from infancy with "Thou shalt and shalt not" ideas in western and eastern societies; even if you are not part of organized religion. Many of these ideas are good; such as do not kill your neighbor. However, many of the religious regulations we live with were arbitrarily imposed a long time ago and remain with us today. Jews and Muslims are forbidden to eat pork and shell fish but can eat beef, sheep and goats. Hindus cannot eat beef. Christians eat pork, beef, sheep and goats. Roman Catholics were forbidden to eat meat on Fridays for many years. Many of those prohibitions had some sound logic behind them originally, but in the light of today's science have no foundation.

Some religious prohibitions have retarded our progression as thinkers. It was not long ago when Galileo was condemned for theorizing that the earth was not the center of the universe. Today creationists argue that men and dinosaurs coexisted. Others argue that their religious texts were not only inspired by God but also are literally true; therefore, they cannot be challenged on the basis of facts or logic.

Male Superiority

In the beginning the female principle was keenly observed by our ancient ancestors. The mother principle was the focus of a divine vision because that's how life works. Mothers and females were part of the religious hierarchy. Towards the end of the Neolithic period circumstances changed. The Mother Goddess was demoted in the pantheon of gods and goddesses. The power of creation and of fertility was transferred from the Mother God to the male Creator God. Finally she was deprived of any semblance of power. In her stead was God, the Father, God the Son, and God the Holy Ghost in Christianity. Her consort and son had deposed her. The most significant result of that action is that of male superiority and domination. God is represented as a man and man is the head of the household by virtue of association.

Male supremacy is a fact of our lives. The idea of male superiority is held valid by most organized religion. The problem for religions is that once they set an axiom in motion it is not easily removed. It is not easy for a Church to say God is not a man, when Jesus Christ is said to be God. Ideas have momentum and religious ideas have staying power. Believers do not want their doctrine to change. They want their religions to have "the truth." Believers need their religious dogma, but at times, dogma gets in the way of social change, scientific advancement and logic. Dogma can create problems.

One of the big issues for churches today is alleging the literal interpretation of a bible or similar book of authority. One hundred years ago many Christian churches were publicly saying that "the bible" was the literal word of God. Today more liberal Christian churches are interpreting the bible metaphorically. It is difficult for most churches to make changes in their beliefs. People want consistency and absolute answers. A church is supposed to provide answers that are absolute and stable. The problem is that churches are now being challenged by logic, reason and scientific advancement.

Churches, whether ancient or new age, use the best logic they can conceive of at the time of formulation. The logic system has a purpose. As an analogy we can use a storyline from a play or movie as a framework for a religion. Every movie has a plot written in a script. The religious script is woven with the intention of telling a complete story. We call the plot a storyline. In most western religions the script/storyline is scripture. It is interesting and no accident that script is the root of the word scripture. The play or movie is either a remake of an earlier production or it is completely new theatre.

An example of religious evolution is Judaism. It gave birth to Catholicism which in turn morphed into Islam, then various Protestant religions which in turn have given birth to the Mormon religion. Each progression was extremely tumultuous and violent. As "new age" religions emerge, they take some of the old ideas and incorporate new teachings into their dogma.

The purpose of a church is to explain, entertain, exonerate, exhort. There is a director, cast of characters and a complete assemblage of production workers. In addition there are props and costumes and endless dress rehearsals. Followers are always getting ready for the big show, which never quite arrives. The Church has the best projection

CAN GOD BE A *Woman?*

system for its movie; it is a picture in your mind. It is portable and customizable for each person. The religious movie plays simultaneously with the ongoing theatre called "Your life". This has been a winning script since the beginning of human history.

More than any other institution in our history organized religion has kept women oppressed. Most major religions, today, are formulated and dominated by males. Through religion, male ideology is dispensed into all of our institutions in society. From the power of the pulpit the male paradigm of superiority permeates almost all organizations in society even female groups. Male superiority is given sanction by the church, because of the idea that God is a Male. Until recently it was commonly accepted by almost everyone, that males were supposed to dominate females. "Father knows best." The Bible says man was made in God's image (Genesis 1:27) and the interpretation is God wants men to be in charge.

Many organized religions foster the idea that women are second-class citizens and attribute that belief to God. Eve is responsible for man's original sin and downfall. Eve attracted Adam with her sweetness and appealed to his lower appetites. Eve tempted Adam into accepting the knowledge of good and evil. Women have an allure men cannot resist. Therefore, women are temptresses and the cause of the downfall of man. The bible also says women are punished for mans downfall. She is unclean during her menstrual period and should defer to men as head of the household. Judaic/Christian dogma frames these ideas.

In church hierarchies where power lies women are excluded. Women are just now entering the "priesthood" in some denominations in limited numbers, but so far most traditional religions have kept them out. In an ironic way women are responsible for man's downfall because they did not keep the reins of power that they shared with men long

ago. If females had kept an equal share of power from Neolithic times forward, this would be a much different and better world. The male structured church took the power away from women by applying brute force against them in post Neolithic times. A female God was supplanted by a male God.

A world with both men and women in partnership would be more caring. In a real partnership we would care more about how the trees breathe and the seas live. The ball is in the women's court now to correct this imbalance. Men have to be awakened and share power with women. Women must wake up and take their share of power. It can be accomplished in very practical ways. WouldArt will encourage voting for female as the vehicle of transformation.

The Words of God

As noted earlier the "words of God" in spiritual books do not always make sense and can conflict with one another. The word of God, in the Christian Bible, Muslim Koran and Jewish Torah are not clear on many issues and needs to be interpreted. These religious texts are purposely complex and confusing in order to avoid giving clear answers. For example, according to most of the world's religions mankind is the centerpiece of God's creation. We are God's chosen people, and we are in charge of the Earth. We are also the apotheosis of God's creations because we are made in His image.

Logic tells us that this cannot be so because we are such a small part of creation. If one thousand books represented the history of the Earth, human's part would be a page or two in one book. In other words, humans have occupied much less than one thousandth of one percent of Earth history. If we extend the analogy to the known universe man's contribution is not even an exclamation point! The entire earth is a speck of dust in our galaxy. Our galaxy is a speck of dust in the greater universe. In the greater universe, Earth, is something less than an electron in the outer rim of an obscure atom. What does that make one of six billion people on this Earth? The insignificance of people, and especially any person, defies mathematical comprehension! We are just part of creation, a very, infinitely small part, not the centerpiece of it. Perhaps we are driven to tell our selves stories of our own exaltedness and glorification because we know deep inside that we are insignificant, but we don't want to be.

Religious leaders defy logic and tell us what we want to hear. "You are special and important to God. God loves you and wants you to live forever in a heavenly state." That is comforting. However, most religions add the following. "If you don't follow God's laws as interpreted by your religious leaders, you will burn in hell for eternity." This is not comforting and not realistic, especially if you have not kept their rules rigorously or are considering breaking them.

What about other beings, monkeys, horses, sheep, dogs, etc? Does God want to keep them in heaven forever? What about bugs? Does God have cockroaches and scorpions in heaven? Are there mosquitoes and leaches in heaven? Do sharks go to heaven? Do tomatoes go to heaven? Is heaven only for humans? What do mosquitoes do in Heaven? In very short order Heaven becomes an extremely complex place to envision and define. The idea of Heaven is a problem for a free thinker.

Patriarchal – Deceit – Zeus

If God created all things, would not God have the power to be all things? Do we limit God because we cannot really

imagine unlimited power? It seems absurd and funny that we presume to know what God is. Religious leaders and sacred books tell us stories about how God behaves. We, as humans, are infinitesimal in the scheme of things. Yet we are quite willing to define what we cannot see and cannot understand or be. Religion's job is to provide answers, absolute answers. If religion did not provide absolute answers and settle nagging questions, it would not be doing its job. The answers that religions provide are not required to be logical or to be proven. They are simply required to be authoritative. The religious point of view is to be taken as gospel.

Religion's job is to answer the questions which cannot be answered. Religions are constructed to convince us we have arrived at the absolute truth. The answers they supply are a blend of truth, practicality, conjecture, contrivance, and falsehood. Whatever it takes to be successful and sustained, religions will do. Religious leaders and followers have lied, cheated, stole, plundered and murdered to sway others to their beliefs and to stay in power. History is filled with such examples as the crusades, the Inquisition, holy wars and internecine warfare between the Shiite and Sunni followers of Mohammed.

Philosophy usually asks many more questions than it answers. Most people do not like philosophy because the absolute answers are far and few between. Religion is different from other branches of philosophy because it arrives at conclusions whether they are true or not. Religion is philosophy that has definitive answers – a special branch of philosophy.

With only males in power, our perception of reality is not in balance. We cannot change the power structure unless we change our spiritual beliefs that God is male. Five hundred years ago Galileo was almost executed by the Roman Catholic Church because he dared to say the Earth

was not the center of the universe. It took more than an additional five hundred years for that church to admit that it was wrong. We do not have five hundred years for males to yield power.

We should modify religions. Religions do not need to answer all questions. Do we need miracles, prophets, messiahs and a profusion of regulations and complexity? Our existence on this planet and our own consciousness really is mystifying and profound. If we cherished each other and followed the golden rule, we would not need another guide for our behavior.

Most people do not feel comfortable challenging the authority of their churches. It is too much work. It is much easier to go along with an established religion with ceremony, ritual, pageantry, pomp and circumstance. In general they do not want to change.

New Age religions are doing a booming business. One can find comfort in knowing that at some point all religions were new age. Even the religion that considered Zeus to be the father of the Gods on Mount Olympus was a new age religion at one time.

Churches do change over time because they want to protect their interests. Protestantism was a radical movement protest of the status quo. Now it is the status quo. If your constituents don't like what you are doing, change is inevitable. Pastors and priests who have angered their congregations eventually are pushed out of their parishes. It happens all the time.

Churches can lose their credibility. The Roman Catholic Church has lost a lot of its stature recently because of the scandalous behaviors of homosexual priests and their attempts to cover them up. This issue speaks about the arbitrary structure of the church and its rules. Priests and nuns are expected to be celibate because church leaders accept the interpretive remarks of Paul in the New

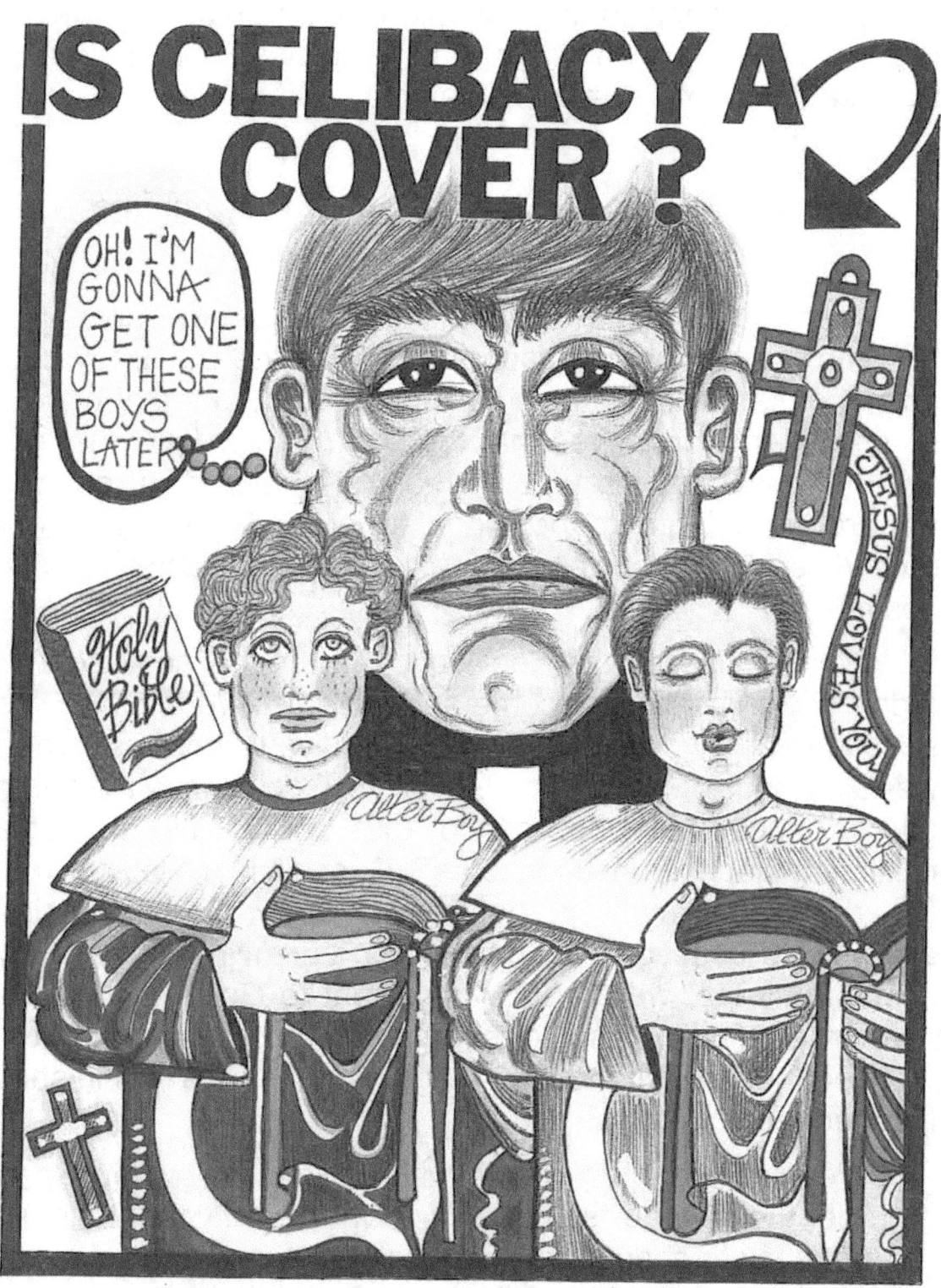

Testament and their belief that a priest should be a father to all and no one specifically. Considering the number of homosexual priests in the Catholic Church and the law suits that have resulted in church bankruptcies, this theory or practice does not seem to be working.

Reward - Multilevel Marketing – Programming

Man is the most manipulating and powerful animal of his time just as Tyrannosaurus Rex was the most powerful animal of its time. We have convinced ourselves that we are so special in God's eyes that there is no possibility that our own hand will obliterate us. In many of the world's religions we are considered to be sinners here on Earth and our reward is not here while we are alive but rather it is in heaven.

Christianity tells us the world has to be destroyed in order for the messiah to come and save us. We think we are so unique and worthy that God cannot live without us. When we talk about ourselves in relation to God, doesn't it seem odd to suggest that God cannot exist without us? Is God's fulfillment dependent upon ours? Doesn't logic tell us that our divine fulfillment is dependent upon God? Religion attempts to assuage our fears about our own existence by assuring us that we are very important to God. However, a moment's reflection should reveal that God doesn't need us; we need God! What most religions teach us diminishes independent thinking.

People are paralyzed with insecurity when they consider their own existence. Our own mortality frightens us. It is not easy to change religious beliefs even when we know deep inside that they are fallacious. God did not create us in its image. We created God in our image – a male image.

What has been designed for western man in Judeo-Christian theology is not logical and impedes our progress as a species. Judeo-Christian theology was designed by desert sheep herders thousands of years ago. It is taught to children of all ages today with great conviction and fervency. Its purpose is to extract allegiance, conformity and conscription.

For example, my daughter attended a daycare at a local church. Once a week they would bring all the toddlers into the church to visit with the pastor. He would tell them stories. One day my three-year-old returned from daycare and told us her "real father" was in heaven. To say the least it was a shock and a wakeup call to us, the parents. At first we laughed; then we realized we had to counteract that programming. We still talk about it many years later. The real point here is how powerful early learning is. In general churches want young children in their congregations. The mind of a child is vulnerable and easy to manipulate. Once a child accepts a belief, it is very difficult to change it. Many churches are masters of probing for and creating fears and anxieties in children as well as their followers in general. Then they offer salvation and threaten damnation.

Although many fine moral ideas are taught in churches and various religious texts, one of the objects of a church is to get its members to stop thinking. Churches do not want any contradictions or objections to its particular theology and methodology. In other words, parishioners should be good sheep. Churches want members to follow its rules and believe its doctrine. The priest, rabbi, shaman or spiritual leader is a shepherd and God's representative. The guild of the priesthood is very special in the human tradition. The mold was cast long before Moses and Aaron became the only ones able to talk with God. The church sets itself up as the sole representative or franchise through which its followers can reach God.

The church is central in many civilizations. This position bestows immense power in the hands of a few over the entire civilization. The influence of the church and church doctrine reaches every part of life. However, the church can make a mistake, and when it does, we all pay the price.

It has been said, "Religion is the oldest con game." Churches convince their followers that they are concerned with their spirituality and salvation, but in reality are more concerned with making money and getting power. Like shell game operators who rely on misdirecting the attention of players while taking their money and confidence, churches require their believers to think about eternal damnation and salvation while putting their money and confidence in the collection plate. They play on fears and insecurities and offer shelter from the thoughts they implant and nightmares they instill.

Religion is a remarkable business because its products are ethereal. The product does not exist in the physical world. The product is a combination of advice, prohibitions, consultations, rituals and promises. All of these are created and collected by individual religious leaders and passed on to succeeding generations who in turn add to the collective body of religious doctrine and keep the business going. This is the perfect business because the need is never satisfied and the demand never diminishes. Religious leaders are particularly adept at pushing buttons at opportune times and reminding their followers of their insecurities and need for answers, admonitions and advice.

Recently Billy Graham passed the reigns of the church hierarchy on to his son who has been less than pious and responsible in the past. That action tells us Billy Graham cares more about his family business dynasty than the quality of his church. Billy Graham is a true master of the pulpit. I saw him preach to more than 20,000 people in Albuquerque in the mid 70's. I could not believe the power he exerted over that huge mass of people; it was hypnotic. He could have asked for human sacrifice, and he would probably have gotten more than a hundred volunteers! The power the man wielded was enormous.

The business of religion never goes out of style no matter how people are doing economically or politically. Religions continue to thrive and expand. If times are good – "praise the Lord". If time are bad – "your reward is in heaven".

Most religions offer canned answers to philosophical questions. These religions are not in the business of perfecting themselves, but preserving themselves. Religions want to preserve power and authority over their flocks and extract a predictable tithe at regular intervals. They are basically businesses!

If you think about it, religions are really the first multilevel marketing organizations. A member is signed up to a particular religion by a parent, friend, preacher or someone else and charged to find other people to join their down the line. Then the religious hierarchy and membership helps the new member to convince other people of the wisdom of also joining. The compensation offered is the assurance or protection one receives from the umbrella organization. The questions that may have bedeviled the initiate are answered. A social network is provided that may also function as an economic network. Religions use network marketing to propagate themselves because it is a great system that works.

Some organized religions have or still restrict scientific research. Take for example stem cell research. Religion says don't create life or do research into the creation of life; only God should do that. Don't play God. A thousand years ago they taught the world was flat, and unbelievers were burned at the stake if they said otherwise. They also taught the sun moves around the Earth.

You may laugh about a flat earth or a sun moving around us now, but limiting or trying to hold science back is not a joke. The current government of the United States which is influenced by main stream religious thinking has restricted stem cell research and genetic engineering. These restrictions are from the middle ages and doomed to eventual failure and ridicule. If religious policy holds, and we cripple this research in the United States; it will happen in more enlightened countries. The point is, science will move forward.

Organized religion knows that it deals with our deepest fears and concerns. Preachers often refer to themselves as shepherds. The church has a privileged position as a primal confidant. The church embraces us on many different levels: social, psychological, spiritual, economic, and historical. Religion calms our nerves about our deepest insecurities and lays to rest our fear of the unknown. As a result we support our churches with money and votes. We give churches an incredible amount of money and allegiance. In return our churches tell us we will live forever and be taken care of in the hereafter, if we follow the rules of our church. This is a very good business deal for the church. In fact religion is the perfect business. They tell people what they want to hear and charge them for it. Religion does more than just calm fears; it also incites anxieties. It reminds followers they are mortal and what is in store for them if they follow the teachings of their church or don't. It does this so that their followers will be good sheep and follow the flock. Religion uses guilt, peer pressure and many tricks of the persuasion trade to keep its people coming back for more and more programming. Religion is salesmanship par excellence.

A friend of mine died prematurely of natural causes and left a wife and two children. At the funeral the preacher was extremely powerful in making sure everyone felt the insecurity of existence. He was very skillful in pointing out that life is fragile and uncertain. He went on to make a very strong case for preparing now for the eternal ever after. Members of the congregation felt weak at the knees. There was crying and wailing and most everyone was putty in this preachers hands.

The power of the pulpit at a funeral can be overwhelming. Talk about striking while the iron is hot. The preacher shaped a lot of thinking that day. Business was probably much more brisk in the weeks that followed. Interestingly, this was the same preacher that told my three year old her "father was in Heaven".

Messiah – Golden Rule

Religious programming has a powerful influence on the way we conduct our daily lives. For example, one of the most important concepts in Judeo-Christian theology is the idea of a savior or messiah. It sends a message to human beings that God created them imperfectly. God then needed to fix that mistake at a later date by sending a messiah to be a sacrifice in order to open the gates of heaven. A messiah presupposes we are not capable of solving our own problems and God designed it this way intentionally.

This is a very powerful message which we give ourselves and are all pressured to believe. We are asked to believe an omnipotent being created us imperfectly, so it could send an incarnation of itself at a later date to save us. As an analogy we could say that a loving potter purposefully makes a defective pot; gives the pot consciousness; then tells the pot don't worry I have a plan to come back later and fix you. Do you have to be a crackpot to believe this story?

The "messiah script" portrays God as hardly being omniscient. The salvation plan is not only illogical it suggests God needed human sacrifice as a means of fixing a mistake; a mistake that it created in the first place. The religious leaders, desert sheep herders, who constructed this story a long time ago, established a sense of inferiority and inability that still exists today in believers.

In order for the Messiah to come, Adam and Eve had to eat that apple in the Garden of Eden. They wanted the knowledge of good and evil. And because they wanted knowledge, they were defective. This defect (inquisitiveness) requires the sacrifice of a messiah. Is it a coincidence that the Church labels inquisitiveness a defect? No.

A useful way of looking at the concept of the Messiah is to play God and analyze the storyline. Let's suppose for a moment you are God. You choose one of your creations, the carpenter ants, to incarnate yourself among. You so love the carpenter ants that you are willing to live among them. You think they have divine potential. You so admire their behavior characteristics that you want some of them to live forever as ants with you in heaven. You think an effective teaching method is to let them brutally kill you. Then you come back three days later and tell them you died for their sins. Who is lacking in finesse and subtleness here, God or the story teller? The story of a Messiah has human inventiveness and insecurity written all over it. The story of the Messiah depicts God as a buffoon that has not made up its own mind. The concept of a Messiah is insulting to God and Humans.

Most religions want people crippled, so they will always have something to sell. Most religions do not want independent thinking. They want their believers to rely on them for what they think. They want people to be like Peter Pan, happy, and to never grow up. If we think for ourselves, we may not agree with religion and may want to modify it. A key theological issue here is determinism. Are we responsible for our thoughts? Do we have volition? Do we have freedom of thought? Are we independent thinkers? Does free will exist?

If we are responsible then we must act accordingly. As a species we are still children because we do not always think for ourselves nor exercise our free will. We do not always act with individual responsibility. Christians, Muslims and Jews appeal to leaders in their religions to tell them what and how to think about God, Heaven and the Messiah.

Having a messiah is like a crutch. We depend upon the idea that a messiah will save us and we do not have to fix ourselves. This translates into many aspects of our lives. For example, many people feel we do not have to worry about the environment because the world needs to be ruined so that the messiah can come and save us and presumably the environment. Many people neglect important aspects of health because they expect to be sick and die and then be resurrected and go to heaven. Ever see the bumper stickers gleefully alluding to "the rapture"? Most of us are looking for someone or thing to take care of us: Lottery tickets, social security, insurance policies, inheritance fantasies, Prince Charming, etc.

Our movements are inhibited and our propulsion is tethered to the idea that a savior is on the horizon – the ultimate sugar daddy. Having a savior means we need to be saved. It also means we expect to fail and that we are unworthy of our own success. We have to fail in some capacity in order to be saved. We are programming ourselves to be failures in order to be saved. The savior concept is very powerful. This is a planet wide neurosis. We all want to win the lottery. We all want someone to take care of us. We all want Prince Charming to show up. We all want the Cinderella story to be true - personally.

The idea of a messiah is appealing but it is a narcotic and a pipedream. It pervades the thinking of Jewish believers who maintain he is coming. Christians, on the other hand, believe he arrived two thousand years ago, and is coming back. Muslims also believe a Messiah is on the

horizon. It has dominated the thinking and actions of believers for thousands of years. The amount of money and allegiance believers put into their religious systems that feed them the messianic story is extraordinary. The allegiance is even more extraordinary and absurd than the messiah story itself. Truth really is stranger than fiction.

What do people want from religion - shelter from insecurity, life after death, ethical and moral structure for life? Most religions deliver these goods. However, there is a price to pay; every business transaction requires an exchange. Remember the cartoon Popeye and the character Wimpy? "I'll gladly pay you Tuesday for a hamburger today." Doesn't religion play the same role? Most religions tell us that our problems will be taken care of, that we will live forever and that God loves us. They promise us "pie in the sky".

When churches say that Jesus is going to "wash away your sins," it means you do not have the power to forgive yourself. Religion has created a spider's web in which people get stuck with their own fear and guilt. Religions want people to believe they cannot free themselves of sin. That is the reason for confession. Preachers forgive the sins of their parishioners by claiming they have been given the power to do so by God.

Guilt comes with the territory of sin. This very successful combination is what most religions use to trap their people. If people cannot free themselves from sin and guilt, they must look to an external source for help. Most churches are expert in playing the guilt trip on their parishioners.

When Jesus was asked: "Teacher, which is the greatest commandment in the law?" he replied: "Love the Lord, Thy God with all your heart and all your soul and with all your mind. This is the first and greatest commandment. The second is like it: Love your neighbor as yourself. All the law and the prophets hang on these two commandments."[4] That is the golden rule. God and everything around you is your neighbor; love your neighbor as yourself. Love yourself, and you love God. Fill yourself with love, and God is manifested in you. God is love. This is a complete philosophy and religion. This is Christ consciousness in action. It is simple but not very easy for most of us to follow.

Christ consciousness is deceptively simple. It is easy to understand "love your neighbor", but it is very hard for most people to follow. People may agree it is a good philosophy and should be followed, but they do not treat each other with love consistently. We do not love our neighbors probably because we do not love ourselves consistently. This is the heart of the human struggle with insecurity and doubt. Love is closely related to self-esteem. They are mirror reflections of each other. Self-esteem is directly related to the capacity to love one's self. The ability to love others is a function of self love.

A good start towards self understanding and changing for the better is to slow down enough to appreciate and accept responsibility for our own actions. Responsibility requires thoughtfulness. Thoughtfulness is required in behavior modification. If the world is to change, people must understand where we are now, and then, where we want to go. Know thyself is the mantra that encourages us to change, stretch and grow.

For most humans thinking about God is uncomfortable because it makes us feel insecure. We are not sure if God likes us. Perhaps God thinks of us in the same way we think of flies. Did you know the house fly cannot eat solid food, only liquids? When a fly lands on a pile of manure, it regurgitates digestive fluids onto the manure to liquefy it. After the manure is rendered liquid, it is ingested or re-eaten. Then the fly lands on your plate and shares its past meals

---

[4] Matthew 22:36-40 Holy Bible, New International Version 1978

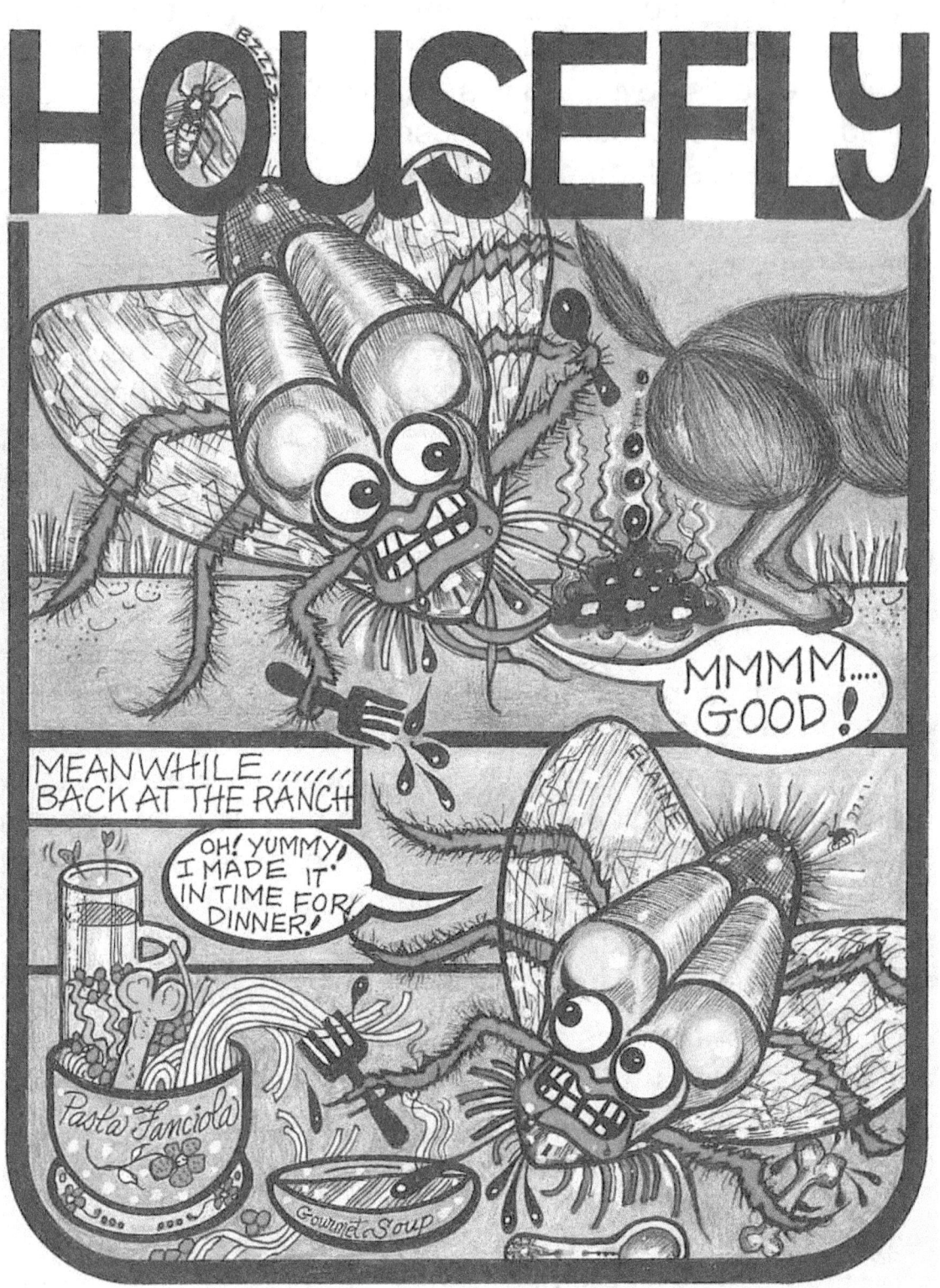

with your present meal. Most people would say the fly is a disgusting, icky, filthy creature. Most people would say the fly is inferior to us and deserves to be eliminated. After all they are disgusting pests.

Flies have a place in nature. If we could talk with a fly, it would probably say that its behavior is not disgusting but natural and enjoyable. The fly would also probably say God designed it to be "the way it is". Does God think the behavior of human beings is disgusting? In the grand scheme of things the Supreme Being might think of us as filthy little creatures that are cruel and not very intelligent.

Religions say God placed us at the top of the food chain on this planet. We may not be. It is also quite possible we are not the only sentient beings in the universe or inhabiting this planet. I hope we are not the most intelligent beings God ever created. I am going to go out on a limb here and say God can do better.

There are those who believe we do not have free will. The argument says we are preprogrammed by a supreme being. That we are just caught up in a chain of events beyond our control. It is fate that determines our happiness or unhappiness not our own actions. The idea is that all events including human action are ultimately determined by external causes. Human beings simply react to the stimuli of their environments. We are no more responsible for our actions than house flies. Philosophers and scientist call this form of argument determinism.

The other side of the coin is that we have freewill and are responsible for our actions. These are two sides of the fence that separates our views of who and what we are. Most of us are either on one side of the fence or the other, and some of us straddle the fence. Many believe free will exists and that we have the ability to make choices. Many believe things are determined for us. Some believe both. What do you believe?

The point of asking these questions drills to the very core of our existence. We are charged with formulating an answer. Are you reading this book because external forces demand it? Or have you made a choice to read here – now? This is not just an exercise in philosophy; it is an affirmation of how you manage your life. The answer is important and it counts.

Another reason the freewill answer is important is that it relates to God. Can we define God? Most religions do. Is it valid to define God or presumptuous? This is probably the most important question we ask about God, because the answer defines us. If we say that God is male; there is a lot of baggage that comes along. We have discussed these issues in some detail. However, one point we have not mentioned very much. If God is male; it is also a God of war.

The God of Abraham is a jealous God. The reason for framing this God as jealous; is so it can "smite its enemies with an iron fist". A jealous God is also God of war. This is a tangled web from which we must extricate ourselves.

If human beings are going to evolve, we must eliminate our ultimate conception of a God of war! War can never be eradicated if it is sanctioned by God. If we do not vehemently state that a God of war is invalid; we will not have the possibility of peace. Peace will only be attained; when a God of war is no more. Have faith and always remember "the pen is mightier than the sword" - any sword.

Chapter Seven

WouldArt Agenda

The Female Agenda

Women must become a more potent political force in the world. This means at least half of the people elected to political office should be women. It is primarily through elected office that women have access to power. Why focus on elected office first? Government is the key for changing other institutions - business, organized religion and educational. Additionally, and most important, elected office is accessible. When women get hold of political offices in equal numbers with men – an important phenomenon will take place. Women will become more credible and respected leaders, and the phenomenon will spread. When that happens, everything will change in all quarters of society.

It is possible for women and men to place female candidates on the ballot for every elected position in the United States. It is important that women run for every office in government from the city council, board of education, congress and the presidency.

The mechanism exists within the established political parties for equalizing the elected gender base here in America. If it is proven to be beneficial here, it will spread to the entire planet. This does not imply that women should dominate politics as men have. The goal is true sharing of political power with at least 40% and no more than 60% of elected officials either female or male. The stage has been set and history is waiting for a gender change in the course of politics. We need to take our planet to another level of government - management.

In a recent movie a hero/warrior states "...focus determines your reality." An idea is like a sword, and if that idea is honed on the strop of truth, it will be very difficult to

resist its cutting edge. The task is to focus on creating a world where men and women are political equals.

Ideas rule and alter history. When people implement ideas they can shatter an existing reality or create a new reality. A change of focus can determine a new political reality. Our focus must be on placing women in all political offices in equal numbers to men. Governments rise and fall with the will of the people.

Economic, political, and even military institutions persist because they have legitimacy, and that legitimacy comes from the perceptions and ideas people hold. People give legitimacy first to ideas then, institutions, and institutions rise and fall because of ideas. The most powerful force for change in history is not the military or money - but ideas. Great changes happen when an idea matures, when it achieves acceptance and legitimacy. The fall of the iron curtain in the USSR was not accomplished by a military maneuver, but by the idea of democracy. China is in the process of changing because it is being seduced by the idea of capitalism. There are many encouraging signs in the political landscape today.

However, not all conditions paint a rosy picture. There are also profound negative forces at work to bring the civilized world back to the middle ages. The fastest growing religion in the world is Islam. The Islamic world is being pressured by radical fundamentalism. Islamic fundamentalism has zero tolerance for female political and power sharing aspirations. This is a major problem for us all today. It is not going away, in fact, it is getting worse.

Everyone must become aware that women are urgently needed in the decision-making processes of all our basic institutions - government, business, religion, academia, medicine, etc. For some people this means just informing them that women are missing from positions of power; other people require more sustained contact with the logic surrounding gender oppression and the benefits of

egalitarian politics. We must build a consciousness of gender awareness at the grassroots level to create the inertia and reality of equality by using the appeal of reason.

Any point of view has the potential of reaching a state of "critical mass" in a society when that idea becomes accepted by a significant segment of the population. The idea of critical mass requires a dedicated minority to lead the majority of people to acceptance of the new concept. The concept of critical mass is a statistical notion that means when 5 to 20 percent of the population believes in an idea or accepts a practice, it is inevitable that the greater mass of the population will accept the idea in time.

Time is always an unknown variable; however, the inertia of an idea accelerates over time. We are very close to critical mass on the issue of politics and women. The fact that two women senators were elected at the same time in California marks a turning point in the attitude of both the male and female electorates in California. We must continue to improve the position of women in order to reach a state of political equality everywhere. We must continue to push the WouldArt agenda forward in order to obtain the critical mass necessary for women to become equal in political power. Now is the time for women to emerge in politics.

Political equality is the key that will allow gender justice to take hold in society at large. Political change is the leading edge of social transformation. Women's equality in politics can create dramatic changes in other areas of society. Given the impetus women can choose to vote themselves into elected office with the help of a sympathetic male vote. A significant minority of male voters will support women candidates and their numbers are increasing. When women vote themselves into office and become true partners in politics, they can create legislation that will change the rules under which the other institutions of society operate. This means greasing the hinges so that the doors of power can be opened in all the institutions of society. Additionally, when women are elected and perform well in political office, all of us will gain more confidence in women leaders.

Political power can transform the operational rules by which all institutions function, but political equality does not immediately translate into equal opportunities across the board. When women assume a full share of elected offices, the doors of the executive suites in business will not automatically be opened wide to accept them, nor will the pulpits abruptly become feminized. It will take legislation and lobbying over a long period of time for women to reach equality in business, religion, medicine and so forth.

Changing the way people think takes time. Changing the way women think about the power they can wield will take time. The facts are simple: politics responds to votes, business responds to money, and women have more votes than money. Women can change business practices through legislation. Religion responds to social pressure and consensus. It is slow to change, but more women attend churches than men. As women emerge in the political world so will the potential to change religious beliefs and business practices. Women have more power than they think. However, gender equality will not come over night. It is a work in progress that requires evolutionary determination and effort.

Not having adequate childcare is one of the biggest blocks women face in accessing political, economic, medical and religious power. Because women realize the importance of child nurturing; they have always assumed the task of child rearing. As a result the self-sacrifice of childcare holds many women back from more proactive self-development. If good and affordable childcare were made available at our work places, both mothers and fathers would be able to have more contact with their children during the workday. Women and men would be able to respond to the minor emergencies children always have and could still hold jobs. They would feel better about themselves as parents and as workers because of a supporting structure to do both jobs.

The fact of the matter is that in most instances we have to do both jobs anyway. So now the goal is to find a way to do them both well. Women are more aware of the dynamics of childcare than men. If women were in political power, childcare would be addressed in legislation.

We need to bring the female mindset to the political table. Women have a responsibility to exercise their full political power and take control of their own destiny, and in so doing change the formula of the male-dominated political equation. Women are an enormous political force like a sleeping giant with incredible strength. It is time for this giant to wake up, stand up, move about and perform the duties of management and control of the Earth. Women must become true equals and partners on this fragile ship we call Earth. Planetary harmony will not happen unless women balance the political equation. The patriarchal experiment has just about run its course! In fact, it has run off course and is about ready to ground our only ship of passage.

In the last forty-five hundred years women have not had equal say with men. This has been by patriarchal design not by the natural disposition of Mother Nature. Women have made some strides forward in the last hundred and fifty years, but we really have a long way to go to reach true equality.

Some encouraging advancements have taken place lately. Critical mass is happening, but the process needs to be accelerated because world circumstances associated with terrorism and 9/11 are threatening the stability of the planet. We cannot afford to wait until things get so bad that we won't be able to stop the slide towards new world wars and environmental disasters on a scale never seen before.

Women must create political parity and help guide humanity in the stewardship of the Earth. Men who make destructive policies must be stopped. Women and men must start acting as caretakers of the Earth rather than gravediggers. Women gathering in Washington on November 16 and 17, 1981, circling the Pentagon hand in hand, chanted, "Take the toys away from the boys! Take the toys away from the boys!" The mothers of the world need to take political power and turn things around. Since 1981 the military-industrial power has grown exponentially.

Women need to mother all of us because our male-dominated culture has created an unbalanced society and a diseased world. Destructive political and military policies are serious threats to all of us, but some of the most harmful things happening today are a result of big business and the destruction of the environment. Multinational corporations are like mindless giants set upon the land with a single instruction, "Make money!" They have no conscience or regard for the future or for the damage they are unleashing. Corporations are destroying the rain forests, the lungs of the world, at such a level that the fires can be seen from outer space by naked eye. These corporations are male-dominated and protected by male-dominated governments; both only care about their own gratification and short-term visions.

It seems shortsighted and dumb that companies would destroy the physical infrastructure that supports their own industries. A grand sense of irony and denial operates in many companies (lumber, mining, chemical, fishing, etc.), and the only apparent justification for their exploitative behavior is making money. They literally do not care about tomorrow. Where are the values of happiness and conservation for the projected future? Initially conservatism was a philosophy associated with maintaining natural resources, but the thinking of today means getting whatever you can without worrying about anybody or tomorrow. Conservatism today means conservation of the systems of abuse, maintaining the status quo of power groups and methods of exploitation. We no longer have very many kings

in the world, but now we have CEO's and Prime Ministers who serve the same function. We still have the feudal system, but instead of lords of the manor we have lords of the board of directors. The impact of these "lords of the boards" far exceeds the damage done in feudal times. A hundred years ago companies were as negligent as they are today; the difference is that today's multinational corporations have many thousands times more destructive power than their predecessors did.

If women do not step forward and help correct and nurture the imbalances in our thinking and decisions, we may all perish. It may be just a pipedream to think that women will do any better than men, but women have not had the opportunity in many thousands of years. At this stage of the game a feminist experiment is better than the present game plan. Men are not natural nurturers. At the very least it represents hope for a better tomorrow. To continue with patriarchal society is suicidal. It is a shortsighted and narrow-minded intellect that does not see the handwriting on the wall. The structural fabric of our society is breaking down and the Earth is being spoiled, perhaps beyond repair. Women are as responsible for these conditions as men, but for different reasons. Women's role in the destructive process is more neglect than collusion, more omission than commission. Women were pushed to the sidelines and forced to watch men rule. Not interjecting or speaking up louder is the sin of omission of which women are guilty. Men are guilty of the sin of commission. We must move beyond guilt and blame, but in order to look forward and create viable solutions, we must understand our past.

It was the philosopher Kierkegaard who said that the human animal always looks to the future while contemplating the past. Women have allowed men to dominate and distort the world. Fear, intimidation and perceived convenience are some of the reasons that women have not struggled with men for decision-making power and human rights. Women

generally fear and dislike physical conflict. The reasons are clear and logical from the female point of view: "If I am smaller, weaker and bound to lose in a physical conflict with you, then I don't wish to participate." Women are not cowards; they don't like to fight because it is not practical. Practicality is a female forte.

Women are intimidated by men's willingness, even desire, to fight. Does this mean that women must learn to like fighting in order to be on a par with men? No. Women must be willing to get involved in the process in order to fix our world. Women have the potential of addressing and dealing with our world situation, but whether or not they will is another question. Women don't have to become more like men in order to compete for top power jobs. On the contrary it would be a mistake for women to clone themselves in the male mindset.

One of the biggest problems we have is the perception that we must fight in order to solve our problems. The idea that we have to scratch and claw for human advancement is a male-biased point of view and is based in part on a military model of the world. Conflict and confrontation many times produces a solution, but it just as often produces unwanted and unnecessary complications, such as winners and losers. What is fundamentally true in this regard is that our perception guides the methodology of our problem solving. If we assume that we can only progress in this world via catastrophic and cataclysmic dynamics, we will accomplish catastrophic and cataclysmic results. Focus determines our reality. Many other methods can work equally well, if not better, than the win/lose scenario. Any need or deficit can be defined as a conflict of interest or as an opportunity for all interests; it is simply a matter of perspective and orientation – our focus.

Part of the problem in changing society's gender orientation is the inertia that has been established in current modes of thinking. We tend not to tamper with the status quo. However, each individual has the responsibility to overcome the inertia of the status quo. Each of us has a responsibility to contribute to society's growth, but change is not easy. Most people find it very difficult. For example, people who are overweight know it is beneficial to shed some pounds, but it is not easy to do so.

Another aspect of the problem is women's perception that not challenging or vying with men for positions of power is *the path of least resistance* and results in greatest comfort. This is not true. Women buy into this fallacy because they do not want to be involved in a power struggle. However, the consequence of *the path of least resistance* is a distortion in the psychological and social relationships between men and women. This distortion does not permit either sex to perform in public or private functions to the best of their capabilities. Everyone's performance is limited by the array of prejudices and limitations let in through the door of *least resistance*. To reach their full capabilities, women must liberate themselves from the artificial limitations and self-imposed distortions of sex discrimination. They must be able to perceive themselves through egalitarian eyes. This is not an easy task for anyone, and women will have to sacrifice some personal comfort to accomplish it.

People have been living in male-dominated cultures for thousands of years, and they will not change overnight. The programming has been built in deliberately over a long period of time to make us believe that male domination is the natural order of the universe. Part of our challenge is trying to figure out what is the "natural order of things." What should the world be like? Should everyone be happy and fulfilled? Should everyone have a voice and input? That sounds good, but is it practical? No one knows if an equitable world is possible for everyone, but it is, at least, a goal worth striving towards. In the final analysis all we can ask of ourselves is that we do our best. The Golden Rule -

"Do unto others as you would have them do unto you." - would go a long way in creating a better world.

The Golden Rule sounds simplistic, and it is. If it were followed, the results would be profound. All the complexity in constitutional and civil law could be reduced to equal rights and liberty for everyone. It is easy to understand and agree with the concept, but is rather difficult for us to act in concert with it.

When asked what the greatest commandment is, Jesus Christ replied, "to love God and your neighbor as yourself." He said, "All the law and all the prophets hang on these two commandments."[5] The main principle put forth is one of love and respect. Our problem as a species is not being able to follow the simple instructions to love and respect each other. A bumper sticker puts it this way, "Commit senseless acts of kindness, and create random acts of beauty."

Imagine a business world where the Golden Rule was practiced instead of the Rule of Gold. It almost sounds absurd to suggest that business competitors should cooperate instead of working against each other. Our current conception of the business world and the universe is of finite resources and limited markets. However, if treated with care both resources and possibilities in this universe are infinite. We see our world in limited ways because we see ourselves in limited ways.

Problems in the world can either be seen as barriers or as opportunities. If we assume the former, we get the comfort of a defined space but limit our desire to grow and adapt. If we assume that problems are opportunities, our capability and accomplishments expand. As our horizons and technology grow, resources in the physical world and within ourselves expand as well. As we learn to travel off this planet, natural resources will literally become infinite. Even if we never leave the earth, our resources in conjunction with our possibilities are infinite right here, right now. It is only a

---

[5]Bible - Mathew chapter 22, verse 36 - 40

matter of perspective and orientation. We need to implement one of the greatest human resources to change and improve the world, the power of women. Our focus must be on women.

THE ROAD AHEAD

Conservation of the physical world profoundly relates to the management of human resources. Respect for women and the environment are not separate issues, but two sides of the same coin. Our environment is a renewable resource, and so are people. Management techniques relate to people, politics and the environment. Each has an effect on all the other vital institutions of society with regard to the roles men and women play.

Change in any power structure takes time. If social injustice towards women were the only issue, transformation of the power structure could take its time. If we had all the time in the world, it would not matter what we focused on in relation to power. We do not have that luxury because our days are numbered if we do not make fundamental changes in how we treat the environment. Radical social change is required in government and business because we need radical changes in our environmental policy.

No one knows precisely how critical our environmental problems are, but the Union of Concerned Scientists, made up of thousands of the world's best scientists including 99 Nobel laureates, issued a detailed statement on November 18, 1992. "There is an exceptional degree of agreement within the international scientific community that natural systems can no longer absorb the burden of current human practices. Human beings and the natural world are on a

collision course" and "fundamental changes are urgent if we are to avoid the collision our present course will bring about."[6]

Are men capable of making fundamental changes in the environment by themselves? All indications suggest that they are not. The male-dominated power structure has not made any "fundamental changes" in the way business is conducted or government run. It is business as usual as evidenced by the ineffectiveness of the 1992 Rio Summit and Kyoto summit on the environment. Additionally the world has been gripped by a violent mentality lately – Terrorism!

Women are our last best hope for fundamental change. They are not tied to the status quo. They can change the world's course through political transformation. Then they can make changes in the economic, spiritual, academic and other communities of social power. All institutions affect one another, but politics can force radical social change faster than any other social institution.

Women need to clarify their political intention because all of humanity requires a correction of course. The likelihood that men will vote to police themselves is a pipedream. The only group of people with the possibility of getting into political power and doing something different is women. They are our last, best hope for doing something right when they get to the oval office and beyond.

When women have more political power, in all probability they will vote for equal pay for equal work, childcare, and enforcement of equal opportunity and sex discrimination laws already on the books. In addition, they will vote for changes in business and government as they relate to the environment. They have a strong nurturing instinct that logically extends to the environment. They understand the desperate need to change the course. Because they have been excluded from many areas in society by law, policy and custom, women will be more

---

[6]Union of Concerned Scientists, press release on 11/18/92 from 26 church street, Cambridge, Ma 02238

motivated to legislate changes that will create a level playing field for all people.

The transformation of human beings will probably go on forever if we can sustain a physical environment in which "a forever" exists. The challenge for us now is to preserve and protect as much of the physical world as we can at the same time as we accelerate political transformation.

Men Must Change

The Union of Concerned Scientists speaking about the destruction of our environment say, "No more than **one or a few decades** remain before the chance to avert the threats we now confront will be lost and the prospects for humanity immeasurably diminished."[7]   Do you hear the words: "immeasurably diminished"? Male aggression and man's conquering instinct are destroying our nest, the Earth. When men are not waging war on each other, they are waging war against the environment. Men must change their destructive tendencies and share decision making-power with women.

Environmental destruction is a result of aggressive actions by male-dominated multinational corporations. Corporations war against one another and create an atmosphere where destruction seems normal. Some level of competition is necessary for survival, but destroying the environment in the pursuit of attaining economic dominance will eventually kill everything. Ecological and sustaining methods of extracting what we need from the earth are possible without depleting the world's resources.

Male-dominated business looks at the earth as if it were a quarterly financial statement. Business is much more concerned with the balance sheet than whether or not there is balance in our ecosystems. The only long-term consideration for most companies is how efficiently and

---

[7]Union of Concerned Scientists, press release on 11/18/92 from 26 church street, Cambridge, Ma 02238

economically they can exploit a situation before they have to move on to new territory. In the United States and throughout the world, some businesses rape and pillage many of our core industries by destroying the environment in which they operate.

In a fishing town close to my home, the commercial fishermen are significantly restricted from harvesting salmon because they are in such short supply. The reason is that fresh water is diverted from rivers to irrigate Central Valley farmlands and supply water to Southern California, so the fish do not have river water in which to spawn. Farming in the United States has made itself so dependent on pesticides and fertilizers that our groundwater has very high concentrations of these chemicals.

A lot of people have bought or are thinking about purchasing a water treatment system. Many people drink bottled water while hoping it is not poisonous. The point is that we are becoming accustomed to and adjusting for anomalies in the world instead fixing the causes of our problems. On a recent car trip on Highway 1 from Portland to San Francisco, my wife and I noticed that most of the forest visible from the highway had been clear-cut with the exception of a thin strip of old growth trees remaining by the road side, but one could see miles and miles of newly replanted trees beyond the thin facade. The trees are all a single fast growing species – forest diversity is gone!

Male-dominated business looks at Mother Earth, as if it were a possession, an object to be manipulated and controlled. The male mindset sees itself apart from the Earth, not part of it. The male mind distinguishes itself from the totality of existence in order to isolate, objectify and control the world. This is similar to the way some men view women as objects and possessions. By reducing a person, or a tree, or the land to the status of an inanimate object, the male mind finds it easier to control, dominate and abuse the world it sees. Entities: trees, water, land, females and the

Earth are not considered as having self-worth, but only worth something if possessed by someone.

During the Reagan/Bush presidential years, the largest bank robbery in the history of the world took place. Between 500 and 1000 billion dollars was taken by various means from the nation's savings and loans and other financial institutions. All kinds of scams were used: insider real estate deals, construction loans, junk bonds, leveraged buyouts, insurance fraud, and so forth. Essentially no one is being held accountable for the colossal amount of money that just disappeared with the exception of a few scapegoats like Charles Keating who are taking the fall, so that the larger gang of thieves can go free. There will no doubt be a few scapegoats for the current Energy debacle. Those prosecuted are responsible for less than 5% of the fraud. Exxon posted profits of 36 billion dollars in 2005; the largest profit in the history of the world. That's what was reported – how much do you think they wrote off as "expenses"?

How could hundreds of BILLIONS of dollars be lost without any accountability? The only answer that seems viable is that the people who stole the money have to be very close to the people in charge of administering the law. In other words, the business and political power structures are in bed together and protect one another. The whole S&L and energy scenario is a bad joke, but this joke is on us, the common taxpayer who is paying the bill. If one billion dollars in gold were stolen from Fort Knox, what kind of government resources would be put into an investigation to catch common thieves? The old saying is still true that "you can have as much justice as you can afford".

Today, business is the more socially acceptable way for men to conduct warfare. Instead of city-states and nations fighting with each other, we now have local, national and international corporations locked in battle for market share, territory and resources. This different type of warfare produces a different kind of destruction, and the biggest

loser is the environment. Economic destruction is tragic in terms of the human drama, but it is not catastrophic as long as it does not destroy the Earth's resources.

Mankind has become more technologically adept than ever in fouling the planet. If man continues to do business in this manner, we will destroy our capacity for doing business at all. The inevitable consequence of "business as usual" is "going out of business" altogether. We must change the formula for business as usual, because it is too risky to continue the human experiment with only men in charge.

To change the status quo women need to be voted into office. Vote for women. Push for women to be in political leadership. Do your part – support women and WouldArt.

Chapter Eight

Political Control

The Mechanics of political control

We need to change the way we do business on this planet. We have to stop mistreating the environment. We have to realize how churches view themselves and what their relationship is to other institutions and warfare. And we have to understand, most importantly, how governments are run. No small order of tasks. We need to be saved from our own destructive hand. Would art be helpful in saving ourselves? What if we use women as a vehicle to forge an alliance with men? Women in partnership with men could be a practical political force. A whole class of people can assume the role of leadership and compel us all to follow and adjust ourselves. Women in partnership with men are the logical class of people to fix our condition. Fix is probably not the right word, modify our circumstance is really what we want to do. Guide us to a better day. Women will make the changes necessary when they assume equal power because they understand nurturing - we hope! Nurturing more than anything else is what the world needs now. Like the song says: "what the world needs now, is love, sweet love." Females have the temperamental disposition needed to guide us to a new age of enlightenment – sweet love is all we need.

Women have been in compulsory training to acquire humility and develop a sense of service for a long time. My father always said that every circumstance either good or bad had something to teach us. Part of the upside of female discrimination and persecution is the learned characteristics of humility, tolerance and compassion. At this point in time we just have to be appreciative of our options for female leadership. Thank goodness our girls are coming to the rescue.

We need to be lead out of our current morass. The current administration of the Earth by men is not capable of

changing direction. Boys can not and will not lay down their toys willingly – it is just not the way men work.

Women, as political leaders, can forge a partnership with men and move us towards a bootstrap mentality. This mentality is not a religious frenzy and does not fix us over night. Women in partnership with men, is a practical, logical progression for the development of humankind while protecting the environment. Taking care of the earth and its inhabitants is nothing more than applying the golden rule and doing housekeeping. Do we want our species to be made extinct? Do we want to ruin the earth? Of course not.

Let's treat the Earth like we would like to be treated. The struggle between the sexes is clearly revealed in the golden rule versus the rule of gold: power versus compassion; might versus right.

What is the goal of life? Is it to become as rich as you can? Is it to have all the power and money you can get your hands on? Or is it to be happy? If you could have either power and money or happiness, what would you choose? The point is to realize that the goal of life is not some physical destination, but a psychological disposition: to be happy. Money and power is supposed to bring happiness, but it does not much of the time. The struggle for money and power produces unhappiness for a lot of people - a lot of the time. Should we stop trying to get rich? No. But our focus, individually, has to be more than just acquiring wealth and power. Let's be clear about what is the real goal of life - happiness. Part of the lesson of transferring power to women is gaining an understanding and appreciation of the intrinsic value of life. We need to appreciate the value of love and community. And the supportive role money and power plays. We have to keep our eye on the goal, happiness, and not the support system - money and power.

What is the benefit for men in releasing power? The biggest lesson is to learn a sense of balance and vulnerability. There is a great strength in accepting a personal weakness. Men generally do not understand this paradox. Moreover men avoid understanding anything that has to do with personal weakness. Alas, this is a large contributing factor to our current problem. Can men learn? Sure, but this in large part is dependent on both a willingness to learn and having a good teacher. Women need to teach men in the same spirit that they teach their own children – with love in their eyes and heart. This is not going to be an easy task, and it is not a responsibility we can ignore.

The only issue for WouldArt is gender equality. This means we must create legislation that a gender (male or female) will have at least 40% of political positions and no more than 60%. OK, you say – how do we do it? The easy answer is – get involved. What does that mean? Register to vote. And actually vote, but make a resolution with yourself to vote for a woman. What if, you say, women are not 40 % of the ballot? Good point! Now we have to change the ballot and laws. We must get further involved in the election process – on the local, state and national levels. There are good mechanisms for getting involved to change the face of politics:

- School board
- City council
- Local Democrat, Republican, Green, etc, parties
- State Democrat, Republican, Green, etc, parties
- National Democrat, Republican, Green, etc, parties
- And many other fine organizations

However, something is missing in the United States and around the world for women – as it relates to political power. Confidence. Not enough women today have the zeal to go out and seize their fair share of political power. Why? Women still lack the confidence to take charge, take command, take over political control. Things are changing, but it is still a slow process. The problem is we are battling thousands of years of coordinated programming. We have a few women here and there with the guts to get out there and stir things up, but not enough.

Well, you ask, how do we build confidence in women? Good question. Let's answer this question by asking a series of other questions. What is power? How do you get power? How do we alter power? Confidence to rule can be a tricky business. People have all kinds of motivation to be "in charge". Some of the motivation is good, and some of it is not so good. The truth of the matter is that our motivations for having power are never simplistic. Our motivations are a composite of ideals and appetites – both good and bad. The reasonable person tries to strike a balance or bargain with both the higher and lower hungers.

I'll tell you a secret – power does not come from money, position, or affiliation – it comes from within. Real power does not reside outside of you; it is how you feel about yourself – how you think. The power that counts is how you hold yourself. If you feel powerful physically – you are. If you feel intellectually strong – you are. If you think your skill sets (carpentry, poetry, sculpture, cooking, etc.) are worthy – then, and only then, are you powerful. There is only one judge - a very harsh one - yourself. Power must be earned; we must earn our own self respect. This is really not the easiest thing in the world to do. In the final analysis the buck stops at home for all of us. We define what we are and how good we are at it. It is hard to fool yourself. I try it all the time, but I am tethered to a truth pole that is anchored in my brain. I try and run off in all kinds of unethical or whimsical directions, but the chain to the truth stick yanks me back – most of the time.

So how do we build confidence in women? I think it is a three step process. We first understand that we judge ourselves in what we do. Second, we take responsibility for our assessment. This is the tricky part – taking responsibility.

Human beings love to play games and one of our favorites is 'hide and seek' with ourselves. We know that cheating on our taxes is wrong or speeding down the highway is dangerous. But, on the other hand, the government is stupid and I am in a hurry. Right? Or, how about cheating on our spouses or cheating on a test? We always have explanations to ourselves – don't we? I am horny and I don't have enough time to study. The excuses get very creative – most of us are very good at excuses.

Every time we deceive ourselves, we weaken our own self esteem. I am not suggesting that we all obey 'the rules'. That is not my point. What is important is to try to understand and be honest with oneself. If you are going to cheat – ok. Just admit it to yourself. Not being honest with yourself is what weakens self esteem and confidence the most. So, on the path to building confidence it is important to be honest with yourself.

The third step in building confidence is to have some real, tangible skill. The skill must be useful, important and necessary in the world. You have to be able to do something that other people admire – and – you have to admire it too. You may be the world's greatest nose picker, but the world does not necessarily value your skill.

You have to do something that is admirable. Most jobs are humble in nature and that's OK. We can't all be Doctors, Lawyers and Indian Chiefs. If you are a plumber, electrician or garbage collector you will probably have a decent paying job for your entire life. And you will have decent self esteem to go along with your job. However, unless you do something else in life that is extraordinary, you are not going to have the highest confidence and self esteem.

In order to lead other people you must have very high self esteem. In order to have the highest self esteem and be a leader you must be very good at several things. You must be a skilled thinker and speaker. You must be people oriented and be willing and able to have public fights on issues. It is also extremely beneficial to have practical skills like cooking, carpentry, poetry, music and/or other artistic endeavors. It is important to be able to give something of practical value back to the world that you serve. People who have honed their practical skills to a high degree find it easier to possess high self esteem. A master furniture maker, cook or surgeon - find it easier to accept themselves - because the world appreciates what they do. They are told they are useful – valuable.

There is no substitute for positive feedback. If the world does not give you enough positive feedback – you wonder about yourself. If you are not told by the world around you that you are important and doing a good job; it is difficult to maintain a high image of yourself. It is important to feel confident, in who you are and what you do – you must feel it in your heart.

The world is skewed towards making leaders out of male candidates. Women are not as often considered for leadership positions. In fact women are encouraged to see themselves a notch or two below men. This is the problem we have with women today. Most women have varying degrees of confidence in themselves. Not enough see themselves in the highest regard and want to be leaders. Many women look at the odds against them and just walk away in disgust. In addition, a high percentage of women in this world believe they are rightfully second class citizens. A very large percentage of men think women are inferior. Our culture has programmed a second class, subservient image for thousands of years.

We need to change these perceptions. We need to have leadership building campaigns for women! We need to create more environments that help women hone their skills and build their confidence. The world is geared to helping men succeed at the highest levels. We need to alter the mechanics of "who" and "how" we create leaders. We need to have a grooming mechanism that prepares women for leadership at all levels. We need to be much more proactive in finding women and helping them to grow into leaders.

Wouldart has a sole purpose of creating gender equity in politics. Therefore Wouldart is a grooming mechanism that prepares women for leadership. Great, you say, how do we do that? We literally build the mechanism. One of the fields that women have been excluded from is construction – building. Wouldart is a combined word of a verb and noun – Would & Art. It induces a call to action by asking questions. Such as - WouldArt help to create gender equality? WouldArt be fun and powerful to do? WouldArt help us all to grow?

WouldArt involves multiple concepts which are blended together. We engage the world by asking questions that provoke another type of WoodArt. WoodArt is the mechanism that advances the agenda of WouldArt. WoodArt is our vehicle for change and growth in propelling the ideals of WouldArt forward. WoodArt itself is anything creative – woodwork – poetry – music – cooking – websites – buildings – theater – you name it. WoodArt works hand in hand with WouldArt.

Making art builds confidence in the creator when the concept and execution is worthy. Well conceived and produced art is valuable to the world and its maker. WoodArt takes raw materials and people, and forms a partnership. This relationship generates wealth. We also build confidence

in the people we engage. Art is born in the minds eye and made manifest by honest labor.

Woodart encourages people to construct useful, meaningful things, and in the process, builds leadership. The endeavor of WoodArt is to create value monetarily; things of beauty and female political leaders.

Woodart is the creation of ideas and things which enhance the world. WouldArt proposes to teach women how to build, construct, design, engineer communities that teach more women how to be master builders - creators. We physically build communities that have roads, sewer systems, houses, schools, furniture, art, music, poetry – everything that a vibrant community needs. We use the model of our own community to teach more women how to build and be builders - creators. We teach women how to be powerful. And we use our power to teach more women.

When you stand before something beautiful that you have created – there is a quiet excitement, an exhilaration that radiates from your heart. It can be an idea; a small clay sculpture; a song; a wood table; a building. Creations get their life and power from the creator; but they also give back power to the creator through the utilization and observation of others. There really is a symbiosis between the creator and a creation.

You may ask – "don't you need to be really strong to be a builder"? The most important thing to be a builder is to be smart. You must have adequate physical strength and coordination. For example, you should be able to lift 50 pounds from the floor to your waist and carry it up a flight of stairs. You do not need bulging arm muscles to be a master builder, you need bulging brain muscles. A builder is first and foremost an engineer – a practical thinker and doer.

Well, you might ask – "how do you know what it takes to be a builder"? Remember the earlier story of the young man who started building houses at age thirteen? That person is me. I have been a builder my entire life – and – still am today. I love to build furniture, buildings, art, words, electronics, computer systems and networks – I love to build "things". Construction of all types helps me to feel powerful and confident. In building things, I have created many symbiotic relationships. I define the things that I build, but they also define me in return. We live and grow together. I started calling my creations Woodart over thirty years ago. I make artistic things out of a wide variety of materials – wood, steel, concrete, stone, etc. In building "things" I get to chose and define an environment. Defining an environment is powerful. Taking raw materials and creating something of value is thrilling. The dance of creating is born in a vision in your mind and played as an original song. Let's band together, collect resources and build a community that will have a rippling effect on this planet.

WouldArt has been Incorporated in the State of California and has a 501C (3) Non-Profit status with the IRS. The WouldArt community will have many locations. It will be a partnership of both men and women, but committed to helping women to become builders and confident leaders. We want to grow the women leaders of tomorrow. How do we do it – we build them! In our community we will also build ideas, web sites and mechanisms for teaching and moving females into the power structure of the world. We want gender equality! How do we get it? We build!

When something beautiful flows from your mind, through your fingers and is made manifest in reality, the feeling is extraordinary. The feeling of power and confidence can be built. It takes determination, discipline, focus and desire. Each moment of our lives is like a picture that we frame in the eye of our own minds. We build each moment

before us, and we have discretion in the vision we want to pursue. We are the architects of our own vision – each one of us. We are builders – all of us – whether we like it or not. It is important to embrace it, and then work with your powers to manifest a reality that reflects your true desire. The trick in life is to discover what ones true desire is – then work towards it. One of my true desires is to build gender equality in the world.

I would use art to bring about gender equality. WouldArt is dedicated to gender equality. I would use WouldArt to create WoodArt and vice versa. WouldArt conceives a new path towards power. WoodArt is the vehicle to power. We will use WoodArt to roll out our agenda and create a level playing field between the sexes. Woodart is a tool of WouldArt to help bring about gender equality – and true liberty for all.

We of this planet are on a road moving towards a heaven or hell of our own creation. The possibilities are infinite – the reality is the dominate desire. Currently the dominate desire is patriarchal. We must balance the equation with the matriarchal element. We need to reach into our hearts and believe who we are – and that we can become a balanced planet. We can live in harmony with all creation and strive to be happy, tolerant, loving and aware. Diversity will always exist and so will a degree of discord and disturbance. Opposing ideas and disagreements are necessary for distillation and progression towards a refined consensus. Humans are designed with fighting in mind – with each other, between the sexes and most importantly with ourselves. We twist and contort ourselves like pretzels in order to emerge into who and what we are. This is a good thing. Or, at least, it should be a good thing.

Work with WouldArt – we can start small – we can begin with a single project it can be a metaphor for people to meet and grow new skills. We will evolve a new strategy on how to bring about gender equality. We will train women to be builders of many things. We will construct buildings, furniture, music, poetry, websites and all that it takes for a new group of leaders to step forward. If we can build one building – we can build thousands. If we can produce one leader, we can produce thousands. We need millions of new female leaders! We need to shake the world. Let's build them together.

Come dream with WouldArt and wish upon a star, and together we will discover who we truly are.

What we are all charged with in life is to find the allusive balance point. We each have a personal equilibrium and as a species we have balance point. We have entered the age of gender equality in the human experiment. We are engaged in a great struggle to find our balance. No one knows what tomorrow holds for any of us. All we have is now. Make a pack with yourself to promote gender equality – now. Truly believe in the equality of all human beings. Feel in your heart that women are as worthy as men. Then, do something that supports your belief.

Chapter Nine

Payoff

The payoff

What do we get after power is shared with women? No one really knows, because when was the last time this happened? The expectation for gender equality is that our political institutions, environment, religions and business will be more nurturing. At least, that is the hope. But really, what does "more nurturing" mean in politics? It means trying to see the balance point in a whole life picture. The female intellect brings a subtle difference to the table of power. The difference is more of an attitude towards sharing than dominating. At least that is the expectation.

Human beings are funny creatures. Look at any species long enough and they will behave badly or silly in some way. Life is just a big experiment – for all God's creatures. It may be that life is experimental for God too. Consider that the pits in avocados are too big; porcupines can not snuggle very well and jelly fish are messy. We are growing as a species. Look back at the dawn of human settlements, only 40 or 50 thousand years ago, and we have made advances in communication, art and technology. Now is the time to move government forward in human evolution.

It takes courage to do new things. Will we as a species learn to govern ourselves and the planet in a sustainable way? No one knows. Today, more than ever, we should be aware that life is very fragile. Each year species are being eradicated by the thoughtless plundering of the earth. Climatic and environmental changes are making whole areas of the world less inhabitable. We should be further along in development of ecological systems that manage the Earth. It would be the ultimate human tragedy if we eradicate ourselves. Bringing women into the equation has the potential of reversing our journey towards oblivion. Women, we hope, would heal the earth by balancing our needs and desires with those of the environment. Time will tell.

My sincere hope is that all of mankind will become more integrated and aware of itself. And in the process heal itself and our relationship to the planet and each other. I have always appreciated the song "Love the one you're with." It tells us to appreciate what we've got. Look around and dig what you see because it is all that you have.

Life is nothing more than a tangle of feelings. Some feelings are good; some are bad; some are logical and some are strange - off the wall. In the process we try and maximize the good logical feelings and minimize the ones that do not work for us. Think for a moment what that means? "We try." We have the choice. We decide what will happen. We are in charge. We are responsible. We guide our thoughts.

This is the scary part. We reap what we sow. Think about a farmer for a moment and what it takes to be a good one? You have to choose the crop to grow. You have to prepare the soil. Get your seeds and tools together. Plant the seeds at just the right time. Provide for irrigation, weeding, cultivation and pruning. Wait for rain, and watch the seeds grow. In the whole process one of the biggest ingredients is hope. You hope there will be enough and/or not too much water. We need the sun to shine, but not too much. Wind is fine, but not too much. We need those little bugs, bees, birds and worms – but not too much. We don't want volcanoes, earthquakes, mudslides or hurricanes. A farmer really has to do her part, but after a while all she can do is sit back and hope the job was done adequately. And that fortune will smile on her efforts.

Are we choosing the right crop of leaders today? Are we satisfied with the selection of our leader seeds? Are we cultivating a good direction for the future? Do we need to make any changes in our plan – our current path? If you were the head farmer what would you choose? If you had to cast a vote for the next crop of leaders – what would it be? Are these just theoretical questions? NO! We are responsible for choosing our leaders. We don't control

everything; farmers are at the mercy of many factors. But farmers set the stage for their crops, they prepare and take precautions and generally hope for the best.

We are all farmers and we are planting the seeds of our future. Every vote is a seed! Our votes can germinate and grow in a new landscape that creates an environment of gender equality. Take care and plant it well.

Join WouldArt and let's build a bridge to a new future together.

This Is Not the end Or Good-Bye!!!

Let's Meet @ HTTP://WOULDART.ORG